Pimp Your Lesson!

Also available from Continuum:

How to Teach with a Hangover, Fred Sedgwick
The Naked Teacher, Louisa Leaman
The Ultimate Teacher's Handbook, Hazel Bennett

Pimp Your Lesson!

Prepare, Innovate, Motivate, Perfect

ISABELLA WALLACE AND
LEAH KIRKMAN

continuum

Continuum International Publishing Group
The Tower Building   80 Maiden Lane
11 York Road   Suite 704
London SE1 7NX   New York
                            NY 10038

www.continuumbooks.com

British Library Cataloguing-in-Publication Data
A catalogue record for this book is available from the British Library.

ISBN: 9780826496539 (paperback)

Library of Congress Cataloging-in-Publication Data

Wallace, Isabella.
   Pimp your lesson! : prepare, innovate, motivate, perfect / Isabella Wallace and Leah Kirkman.
       p. cm.
   ISBN-13: 978-0-8264-9653-9 (pbk.)
   ISBN-10: 0-8264-9653-9 (pbk.)
   1. Teaching–Great Britain. 2. Teachers–Great Britain. 3. Lesson planning–Great Britain. I. Kirkman, Leah. II. Title.

   LB1025.3.W347 2007
   371.102–dc22

                                                         2007017766

Typeset by BookEns Ltd, Royston, Herts.
Printed and bound in Great Britain by
Antony Rowe Ltd, Chippenham, Wiltshire.

Contents

1 Unleashing the Pimp Within . . .   1

2 Pimp Your . . . Preparation   8

3 Pimp Your . . . Lesson Plan   29

4 Pimp Your . . . Assessment for Learning   42

5 Pimp Your . . . Social, Moral, Cultural, Spiritual
Element   57

6 Pimp Your . . . Every Child Matters   65

7 Pimp Your . . . Differentiation   72

8 Pimp Your . . . Literacy Focus   87

9 Pimp Your . . . Numeracy Focus   94

10 Pimp Your . . . Information and Communication
Technology   98

11 Pimp Your . . . Resources   103

12 Pimp Your . . . Starter Activity   112

13 Pimp Your . . . Plenaries   125

14 Go Forth and Pimpify . . .   139

If a doctor, lawyer, or dentist had 40 people in his office at one time, all of whom had different needs, and some of whom didn't want to be there and were causing trouble, and the doctor, lawyer, or dentist, without assistance, had to treat them all with professional excellence for nine months, then he might have some conception of the classroom teacher's job.

Donald D. Quinn

Nothing strikes such fear into the heart of the overworked, undervalued teacher as the prospect of inspection. Perhaps it is because we feel it often involves being inserted into a dehumanizing four-point scale. What other career was ever subject to being summed up in such a nutshell as this? 'Well, Mr Mozart, much of your music is excellent but some of it is only slightly above the international average; so overall, you're a number 2.' Few of us glow with pride when we are awarded the dubious title of SATISFACTORY; even more frustrating sometimes can be arriving second at the finishing line with a 'didn't-quite-make-it' GOOD. So how *do* we ensure that the much-coveted OUTSTANDING box gets ticked? And why do an elite few keep it such a privileged fellowship? This book will reveal, in detail, the secrets to impressing the pants off your observer, whether it be your head of department (HoD), headteacher, mentor or – worse still – Ofsted!

Teachers tend to be perfectionists. When faced with the gaping chasm between UNSATISFACTORY and EXCELLENT we *could* feign indifference – but who are we kidding? We know we will be there in the staffroom at the end of the day joining in the 'Have you been done yet? What did you get?' ritual. In fact, we probably have a lot more in common with our pupils than we realize – we are all victims of quantitative, positivist data analysis within the school system. We teach to exams. We work daily in an environment where the obligatory testing of children has become so normalized that we consider an 'ideal' child to be one who achieves the designated 'ideal' standard at a specific age. It is hard not to get caught up in the insidious discourse of standardization. The main purpose of an observation should certainly be to enhance our professional development – but sometimes doesn't it just feel like we're taking a test?

We know you're already good. In fact, you might very well already be deemed outstanding by the observation gods which smile their grace upon us. YOU are exactly who this book is for: great teachers who want to put two fingers up and stick out their tongues at any false, uncomfortable, forced observation situation that tries to tell you that you are anything less. We've done all the legwork for you, identifying all the boxes that need to be ticked and giving you practical, innovative ideas to tick those boxes with. We've foreseen the rotten, lesson-foiling, bang-your-head-against-the-wall events that always seem to occur when it's your 60 minutes to shine, and we've given you some crafty cheats to elude them with. We've even put our heads together to identify the mouldy-oldie stale tricks that you need to give a wide berth to. You'll find these in the 'Trash it!' section of the chapters. Last but not least, if you read our book and don't like it, we've given you a handy classroom doorstop and/or shelf decoration.

Please do not be mistaken or spend your hard-earned money if you think this is a lesson-in-a-bag: it's not. There's no smoke and mirrors, Magic 8 Ball or website that you mail away to, to receive your ready-cooked lesson plan. What this book provides is some inspiration, some new ideas, and a fresh look at what to pull out of the bag when your observation time comes knocking. An outstanding lesson is about taking some risks and trying something new. We're not asking you to reinvent the wheel, but you could consider putting some alloys on the ones you've already got. No one was ever told they were outstanding for asking their students to 'Copy the bullet points on page 63 into your book and answer questions 1–9 on page 64'. That guy might not even be satisfactory.

Though you may be tempted after reading this book, don't put it away in a gold presentation box for posterity and intermittent worship. It's good, no, it's *outstanding*, but unlike your dinner jacket and wedding china, it need not be saved for special occasions. In fact, all of the strategies mentioned are perfectly manageable for everyday lessons. We realize that you may not put them together in the award-winning combos or scrutinize the details that will earn you your 'Outstanding' on a daily basis, but throwing a couple of big punches (a flashy starter, perhaps?) on a Wednesday afternoon should not be too big a stretch for the high-quality readership this book draws. Not only that, but these techniques are a little like stew, or spaghetti Bolognese, in that they are often much better after the second or third day. We all know that our students can be suspicious of change and work much better in a routine, so don't surprise them when you need them to be calm, cool and comfortable. Test-drive a few of the strategies that follow before you make your choice about which will suit you best for your observation lesson. You've also got to ensure that your expectations of the class are reasonable; no matter how much you stomp on the accelerator you will never get Ferrari performance out of a Škoda.

We are certainly not suggesting that just anybody can plan, prepare and deliver an exceptional lesson – but bear in mind this is not a survival guide. When we train to be teachers, the focus is usually on how to cope with and solve problems in the classroom, but can any of us remember being trained in how to really excel and impress? We good-old-competent teachers are well aware that good, old and competent isn't enough to hit the buzzer on the new observation scale. Of course, we should assume that an observer wants to ascertain the standard of our normal everyday teaching, but, let's face it, what's the point of delivering one of our normal everyday lessons when we're competing against people who'll be pulling out every stop they can get their hands on. Although no genuine human being teaches like that every single working day, that spectacular, all-singing-all-dancing lesson has become the 'Outstanding' mark against which we are all measured. So, yes, there's really no point in holding back on the bling for fear of overdressing for the occasion.

Not every element of each of these chapters will be suitable for every observation lesson. Your task is to cherry-pick what is best for your class, your topic and your observer's agenda. There is, without a doubt, more than a little something for everyone here and it's up to you to make it your own. Have you ever been to a party where someone shows up in the same dress/shirt/outfit as you (not counting being a bridesmaid, ladies)? It's embarrassing. Same goes for observations: you want to put your own stamp on it and be original in your own right. Imagine your HoD's disdain when, in the fortnight it takes to observe everyone in your department, she sees the exact same starter activity four times! This is precisely why we've given you the mug, and now you have to make your own cup of tea. That being said, nothing would make us happier than seeing an Ofsted report that stated: 'Teaching in the school was consistently of an outstanding standard as there was strong evidence of the use of the revolutionary text *Pimp Your Lesson!* in all subject areas.'

Another thing to keep in mind as you are planning the most exciting lesson of your life, is that there are some things that you need not squeeze into EVERY lesson. Literacy and numeracy can be those tricky, stinky little bugbears that we scratch our heads over and stretch into odd corners of our lesson plans because we feel we have to. This need not be the case. It won't necessarily work in every lesson, though you should definitely include one or the other. Ditto for the 'social, moral, cultural, spiritual' element. Don't feel you have to put something unnatural or forced into your lesson just for the sake of ticking a box. Unless, of course, it is a plenary ...

Perhaps you have bought this book because you have an imminent Ofsted Inspection, a quality assurance observation or an interview lesson to teach. Maybe you are in your training or NQT year and are anxious to stun your mentor with a big, bright, shining star of a lesson to get them off your back for a while. In what follows, we will show you how to hang the flashy accessories on your already effective teaching. You can use this book as a reference when you want to pimp up a particular aspect of your teaching or you can read it cover to cover whenever you're feeling like you've lost your super-powers. Teachers have no time to waste, so our suggestions will be practical and ready to use in lessons across the curriculum, from Latin to dance.

Even the most innovative teachers can find themselves in Noideasville when under the threat of being observed. It's Sod's

Law. We *walk* around happily every day, but if someone told us they wanted to *observe* the way we walk we would become self-conscious and quite probably walk in a less-than-normal manner! You might be working yourself up into a state of absolute terror at the thought of that interview or inspection day, dreading the moment the bell rings to signal the start of your ordeal. If so, then you are joining a prestigious club of decent teachers who really care about their job. When people (who have clearly been living in a box their whole lives and were educated and raised by wolves) ask if teaching really is a difficult job, you must resist the urge to box their ears and scream obscenities at them. What most don't understand is that, as teachers, we put so much of ourselves and our personal energy into the brilliance that we hope to impart on our capricious audience, that it *is* a personal affront when it goes poorly or you are told it is not quite up to scratch. Feel justified, and normal, about being a little neurotic! Never listen to the buggers who tell you that they are not bothered what the outcome of their observation is – either they have never taken *pride* in their teaching, or they are really pooing their pants behind that staffroom table.

Before we go any further, we will quickly deal with your anxieties. What is the worst thing that could happen on the day? You forget all your plans? The pupils play up? The photocopier breaks down (again!)? No. The worst thing that could happen, as a particularly neurotic colleague once pointed out, would be for your trousers to fall down in front of the entire class and the observer. All other potential disasters fade into insignificance before this one. And here's the good news – laws of probability suggest that it is relatively unlikely that your trousers *will* fall down; plus, you could always wear a belt.

It's been only in recent years that 'pimp' has become a part of the vernacular. Now, rather than being an objectionable noun, it has become a dazzling verb, which in all its one-syllable glory refers to the extreme improvement, enlargement and general betterment of something. Anything. Everything. Including your own already-admirable lessons.

We would like to drag this term even further away from its

original connotations, to apply it specifically to the art of teaching. Henceforth, pimp will incorporate four verbs in one – the four most important instructions for any teacher facing an inspection of some kind: PREPARE, INNOVATE, MOTIVATE and PERFECT. What better way to blast yourself into the contemporary, the colloquial, the idiomatic than with this brilliant word and concept. Use it in the staffroom, use it in your classroom, use it when you are making dinner. By the end of this book, there will be no bounds to contain your newly articulated interest in excellence.

So just for a while, put aside your marking, your stress balls and that anxious feeling that always consumes a conscientious teacher before an observation lesson, and let us show you how to be a player in the observation game, and really Pimp Your Lesson! ...

2

Pimp Your . . . Preparation

Good teaching is one-fourth preparation and three-fourths theatre.

Gail Godwin

If you want to win an Oscar, you have to be ready to do some serious preparation for your performance. Renée Zellweger put on three stone; Dustin Hoffman spent time at a psychiatric institution. Although you may have come close to doing one or both of these things by the time your inspection period is over, you also need to follow some imperative steps to ensure your lesson is a hit with the viewers.

Research is key here. For example, if you are preparing to teach an interview lesson at a new school, you need to find out which of your assets the observer is most likely to be checking out. Since you will have no idea of their personal preferences, have a sneaky peek at the school's most recent Inspection Report on the Ofsted website. What have they been told they need to work on? This is bound to be in their school development plan and thus will be forefront in the mind of your observer. Do they have a specialist status? If so, make sure that you work this into your lesson plan. What is the buzz-word or initiative in the school at the moment? Anti-bullying? Learning Styles? Student Aspirations? Raising Boys' Achievement? Can you incorporate this in your teaching too?

Let's begin by dispelling some of those common worries by giving you some decidedly cheeky cheats, including the controversial one about what to do if you are familiar with the class you are to be observed teaching and you know that one troublesome pupil will do their damned hardest to disrupt your fastidiously planned lesson. (Put down that building permit for a replica of Miss Trunchbull's 'Chokey' from Roald Dahl's *Matilda*; we've got a far simpler solution.) Don't let this worry detract from your lesson planning for one moment longer: have them removed on the quiet, to a friendly colleague's room. Your colleague will be only too pleased when you offer to return the favour the next time it is *their* turn to be visited.

Here's another reason to breathe a sigh of relief: it is entirely acceptable (and sensible) to *lie* to your class about why there will be an observer in the room. If you have a fantastic relationship with the class, by all means tell them that it is *your teaching* which is being assessed, but you may regret this when you start to see the anxious, awkward pity on the faces of your pupils if they perceive you to be nervous on the day. And they *will* be looking out for any signs of nervousness or differences in your delivery rather than concentrating on their own work. One colleague, who always had a good relationship with his classes and was liked by pupils for his good sense of humour, lost any hint of a smile when during an Ofsted Inspection, a smart-arse in his top set who was sat next to the po-faced inspector, inquired, 'Aren't we going to play sleeping lions like we usually do, Sir?' Finding himself permanently out of favour after the event, the poor boy must have realized that there are some things you just can't joke about. To avoid this kind of debacle, tell the class that this observer has heard how exceptionally well they have been working and that he or she would like to come in to witness their brilliance first-hand. This takes the awkward focus off you and more importantly avoids the disturbing implication that their teacher is not trusted because he/she has to be 'checked up on' by more 'important' staff.

If this all seems too much like ducking and diving and you begin to feel a guilty obligation to take the moral high ground and skip this chapter, consider this first: it is generally and openly acknowledged that a school facing Ofsted often becomes a sort of obscene theatre in which an exaggerated 'drama of excellence' is played out. Therefore, you can be quite sure that your in-house observer, whether they be subject mentor or an intimidating member of the senior leadership team (SLT), have themselves, on a number of occasions, gift-wrapped their own teaching for the special occasion of observation. Above all, remember this: the observer *knows* that you are *expecting* them, therefore they will view your lesson as an indication of the ABSOLUTE BEST THAT YOU CAN OFFER.

For some truly pimped planning, you need to get inside the mind of your assessor. A good observer will have a clear idea in their head about what constitutes excellent teaching and should most definitely use a purpose-designed observation document that takes account of and allows for easy reference to these standards. Most importantly, the criteria for excellent teaching should be based (obviously) on Ofsted's own descriptors. The observer, therefore, should first assess whether your lesson has demonstrated the eight main indicators of effective teaching and then establish to which standard ('Outstanding', 'Good', 'Satisfactory', etc.) you have shown them. Unless you are superhuman, proficient in blackmail, or have read this book ten times already, it is unlikely that you will score 'Outstanding' in every single category. However, with a majority of 'Outstandings' and just the odd 'Good' dotted about, you should still come out on top overall.

So here is the exam paper you are actually allowed to read before the exam – the eight criteria for effective teaching. If an observer does not refer to these, their judgement was simply never worth pimping for. So refer to these frequently during your preparation-pimping, because, well, you know how you're always going on about the importance of revision ...

Eight criteria for effective teaching

1. The teacher plans effectively and sets clear objectives that are understood

Many observers will make judgements relating to this criterion as soon as they have read your lesson plan – although they will obviously have to wait to see evidence of how well your pupils understand what it is you want them to achieve. The process of creating a perfect lesson plan document is discussed at length in Chapter 3, but the documents that you submit for perusal with your lesson plan (such as pupil information and your intended provision for special needs) will provide further sparkling evidence of your planning perfection.

2. The teacher shows good subject knowledge and understanding

This is a clear reminder for you to plan a lesson that allows you to showcase your subject expertise without leaving your pupils in a demoralized heap of utter inadequacy. Challenge yourself to teach the observer something that they never knew or fully understood before but which is bound to arouse some interest in them. If you can make your lesson irresistible for the observer to become engaged in (without resorting to a striptease), then you are already well on the way to getting that 'Outstanding' box ticked.

3. The teaching methods used enable all pupils to learn effectively

Use your preparation time to perfect your knowledge of the individual needs and special educational needs (SEN) of pupils in your class. A good teacher is of course aware of the special requirements or difficulties of each pupil, but it would be very difficult indeed to remember every child's individual education plan (IEP) and targets off by heart. Swot up on them; highlight them in your planning and show clearly how your lesson will cater for these specific needs.

Take the time to check through class data to remind yourself of the pupils who are underachieving or who could be pushed further. Show in your planning that you have taken this into consideration by, for example, referring specifically to a couple of pupils and flagging up your intention to question these unwitting victims whether they raise their hands or not.

4. Pupils are well managed and high standards of behaviour are insisted upon

OK, so this is the one that is, by definition, most difficult to prepare for because we just don't know what the little buggers are going to do, say or – in the worst-case scenario – throw. However, if you have just found out that you are going to be observed with your very own 'class from hell', do not despair. Take a deep breath, step away from the noose and follow these simple instructions in the lead-up to the observation:

- Spend the next lessons that you have with this class being as happy and endlessly positive as one of Santa's little helpers on Prozac. Tell the class how much you love teaching them, how great they are, how proud you are of what they are achieving. Yes, it is possible to *feign* an appreciation, even for *that* class. Even if it makes you feel really stupid at first and you just can't see it working, the power of positive suggestion is incredible and it will – if nothing else – at least stun them temporarily out of their automatic modes of behaviour. Believe it or not, you may actually find yourself liking them slightly more too because, weirdly enough, through this *simulation* of affection for a class, our underlying attitudes can be fundamentally altered. This leaves us far more open to experiencing for real the positive feelings that were originally merely a façade. OK, we admit it sounds like an airy-fairy, namby-pamby load of tosh, but in our experience it works – so give it a try.
- This one's sneaky. Have you heard of Pavlov's dogs? Use the lessons you have left with this class to plant a clear link in their head between good behaviour and ... chocolate. Award chocolate to those who have been most diligent at the end of a lesson and they will soon be salivating at the mention of hard work. This is a perfectly legitimate motivational technique so you don't need to blush if a pupil refers to it during your observation. Have some chocolate handy – you could even offer a chunk to your observer! Hell – we knew a *head*teacher who paid pupils £20 to behave!
- In a confident and happy way, make sure all pupils are aware that there will be a visitor in the classroom next lesson. It usually works best to present this as a positive opportunity for the class to shine, but if they really are little monkeys you may wish to hint that their behaviour is being checked up on. However, do not convey this in a smug or vitriolic way as you may turn your little monkeys into a herd of raging King Kongs.

5. *Pupils' work is assessed thoroughly*

It would be stupid not to ensure that every single exercise book is marked up to date with useful, diagnostic comments and clear targets. Be wary of that old trick of devising lessons that don't require exercise books so that you can leave that pile of marking at home a few more days. Unless they are really unimaginative or naïve, your observer will know this game and may well have played it themselves when it was their turn to be observed. In doing this, you risk their asking you to provide other on-the-spot examples of your written assessment anyway.

In an ideal world, your pupils should all know what level/ grade they are working at and what they need to do in order to progress. This is becoming an increasingly popular question from inspectors to pupils. To avoid the pupil switching to default mode and answering 'Er ... I dunno', make sure each pupil has no excuse not to know this information by writing it clearly in their books.

6. *Pupils achieve productive outcomes*

The only way you can prepare for this is by laying the appropriate groundwork in the preceding lessons so that pupils are well equipped to produce the sort of work that you are requiring of them. You can, of course, plan ways to highlight their achievements, for example through high-profile question-ing with lots and lots of pointed praise from you ...

7. *The teacher makes effective use of time and resources*

Why is it that as soon as we know we are going to be observed, we try to cram twice as much as we would normally attempt to cover in a week into one lesson? Timing is oh-so important. Too many of us have been in that situation when you are about to finish delivering a great observation lesson, the sun is shining, the observer is smiling and suddenly the bell goes before you've finished the plenary or set the homework. The observer, who had already put down her pen, has to pick it up again and note something negative down about your timing. Consider carefully and realistically how long each section of your lesson will take, remembering to err on the side of generosity because, well, it always takes longer than we think, doesn't it? Be sure to note down these timings on your lesson plan.

8. Homework is used effectively to reinforce and extend learning

Always build the setting of homework into your lesson plan so that you don't forget to do it and never, ever, *ever* wait till the end of the lesson to set it. It is a popular opinion among inspectors now that this is bad practice because it doesn't always allow time for queries or for slow writers to note down the task.

The format for observation used by your establishment may well feature a grid like Table 2.1 (overleaf).

The troublesome aspect of this is that it obviously allows for a very subjective interpretation of what 'Excellent'/'Outstanding' is unless the observer is also required to refer to clear and concise descriptors for each of the standards. The following descriptions in Table 2.2 (page 17) appeared within the 'Guidance on the Use of Evidence Forms' document for Ofsted Inspectors in September 2005: 'Guidance on where to pitch judgements about the overall quality of a lesson'. Inspectors are advised to make a decision about which grade description 'best fits' the lesson they have observed rather than expecting every single standard to be matched.

Table 2.1

Criteria for effective teaching	Excellent	Good	Satisfactory	Development needed	N/A
1. The teacher plans effectively and sets clear objectives that are understood.					
2. The teacher shows good subject knowledge and understanding.					
3. The teaching methods used enable all pupils to learn effectively.					
4. Pupils are well managed and high standards of behaviour are insisted upon.					
5. Pupils' work is assessed thoroughly.					
6. Pupils achieve productive outcomes.					
7. The teacher makes effective use of time and resources.					
8. Homework is used effectively to reinforce and extend learning.					

Table 2.2

Description	Characteristics of the lesson
Outstanding (1)	The lesson is at least good in all or nearly all respects and is exemplary in significant elements, as shown by the exceptional enjoyment and progress of the learners. All pupils are engrossed in their work and make considerably better progress than might be expected. Achievement is very high. Teaching is stimulating, enthusiastic and consistently challenging stemming from expert knowledge of the curriculum, how to teach it and how pupils learn. There are excellent relationships in the classroom. Teaching methods are well selected and time is used very productively for independent and collaborative work. Activities and demands are matched sensitively to pupils' needs. Well-directed teaching assistants, and paired or joint teaching, reinforce and strongly support learning. Non-classroom-based, Key Stage 4 and sixth-form activities such as private study, research and work placements, develop competences very effectively.
Good (2)	Most pupils make good progress because of the good teaching they receive. Behaviour is good overall and learners are keen to get on with their work in a secure and friendly environment in which they can thrive. The health and safety of learners is not endangered. Teaching is well informed, confident, engaging and precise. The work is well matched to the full range of learners' needs, so that most are suitably challenged. Teaching methods are effectively related to the lesson objectives and the needs of the learners. Teaching assistants and resources are well

17

deployed and good use is made of time. Assessment of learners' work is regular and consistent and makes a good contribution to their progress.

Satisfactory (3) The lesson is not inadequate in any major respect and may be good in some respects, as shown by the satisfactory enjoyment and progress of the learners. Most pupils' learning and progress are at least satisfactory. Teaching is accurate; teachers have secure understanding of the curriculum and the teaching of key skills. They seek to make work interesting and varied, and they involve pupils productively. Pupils understand what they are expected to do, and tasks have sufficient challenge to keep them working well, independently or co-operatively. The school provides successfully for pupils who do not respond well to school or who have difficulties in learning. Relationships are constructive and there is sensitivity to the needs of individuals and groups. Support staff are adequately managed and soundly contribute to pupils' learning. Homework extends class learning well. Pupils are given scope to make choices and apply their own ideas.

Inadequate (4) A lesson cannot be adequate if:
- Most learners, or a significant specific minority of learners, make less than satisfactory progress, whether this be due to unsatisfactory teaching or the impact of bad behaviour.
- Learners' overall behaviour or attitudes are unsatisfactory.
- The health or safety of learners is endangered.
- The teaching is unsatisfactory. This will usually cause the learners' progress to be

unsatisfactory, but occasionally progress will be satisfactory in spite of the teaching due to the good attitudes of the learners. Unsatisfactory teaching is likely to have one or more of the following:

- weak knowledge of the curriculum leading to inaccurate teaching and low demands on pupils;
- work badly matched to the pupils' starting points;
- ineffective classroom management of behaviour;
- methods which are poorly geared to the learning objectives or which fail to gain the interest and commitment of the learners;
- inadequate use of resources, including assistants and time available;
- poor assessment.

Did you spot the problems here? There are still significant difficulties presented by bizarre, ambiguous phrases that only Ofsted could come up with. Don't we all have very different ideas about what constitutes an 'excellent relationship'? And what on earth is 'satisfactory enjoyment' ...?

T. Jackson Chizzle began his PGCE four months ago and was fast becoming an excellent practitioner. Having been observed umpteen times by his mentor since his course started, he was not fazed when he learned that his Professional Studies Tutor was making her first trip to his host school to assess his teaching.

Sitting down in the staffroom with a coffee, T. Jackson Chizzle checked his timetable and breathed a sigh of relief when he realized it would be with his A-level class, which would allow him a good opportunity to show off his subject knowledge. Still a week away, he already had an idea of what he would teach for this

> *observation lesson, but, having a fairly enviable social*
> *life, he was well aware that he had a tendency to leave*
> *planning to the last minute.*
>   *T. Jackson Chizzle needed help to ensure that he was*
> *the Prince of Preparation when his tutor turned up.*

Wedding magazines reassure the nervous bride and groom by providing them with a chronological checklist for jobs to be done before the marriage. To help with the countdown to *his* 'Big Day' we advised T. Jackson Chizzle to work through the following stages of preparation.

As soon as you know you are going to be observed

If you are lucky enough to know which class you are going to be observed with, you can begin pimping immediately. Show yourself off to your best advantage: if you had intended to start a particular topic after half term which would lend itself better to the creation of a dazzling lesson, then move it forwards and start this topic earlier than planned.

Deliver the next few lessons with the impending inspection in mind. Give the pupils some impressive subject-specific vocabulary to use a few lessons prior to the observation. This will provide impressive evidence of pupil learning and progress. The class needs to be made familiar with any new, whizzy activities you intend to use in order to avoid a roomful of bemused faces on the day of the observation. However, do not, under any circumstances, direct a full dress rehearsal! Pupils' familiarity with your exciting, innovative techniques is crucial for convincing the examiner that this lesson hasn't been pulled out of a one-off gold lamé panama.

Gather any useful documents. Do your best to obtain a copy of the school's Quality Assurance Lesson Observation form or the college's observation format. This should show you (and the observer) exactly what criteria you need to meet in order for your lesson to be deemed 'Outstanding' in this particular case.

Do some sneaky research. Find out whatever you can about the particular observer's observation habits. The most effective way to do this is to talk to colleagues who have been observed by this person already. DO NOT CONTACT THE PERSON DIRECTLY! Do they have any pet hates? Is there one particular thing they always look out for? Homework-setting? Use of plenaries? On one occasion, a conscientious colleague was devastated to find that, having taught a truly inspirational lesson, the observer had been sitting making a list for her of all the pupils who were wearing illicit jewellery.

Take the time to ensure that you have an attractive and positive classroom environment. Display key words and motivational posters and make sure that displays are breathtakingly pimped up too.

A few days before

Inform the class that the observer will be present. Unless you have an exceptionally good relationship with the class do not specifically tell them that it is you who is being observed (see above).

Prepare to outwit your observer. Put together an impressive collection of documents for their viewing – examples of assessment, your carefully kept mark book, baseline data for the class, a seating plan, impressive resources that you have produced and recently used with this class, special needs information and individual education plans. It is important that pupil data is highlighted and/or annotated to show that you use this information to inform your planning and teaching, and that it doesn't only see the light of day when an inspector calls ...

Make life easier for yourself. Photocopy each resource to be used in the lesson onto a different-coloured paper. This will assist enormously with your organization and distribution of materials on the day, especially if you are feeling nervous and likely to inadvertently muddle things up.

Check the books. Ensure that exercise books are marked up to date and that pupils have been recording homework for your subject in their planners. (You may need to do some damage limitation here, and ask pupils to record homework retroactively.)

The night before

Pimp your image. Set out an outfit that makes you look and feel like an outstanding teacher – it's surprising what a difference this can make. Hunt out your lucky underwear. Leave the gold chains and leopard-skin suit in the wardrobe.

On the day

Take control. Remember, it is your classroom and you have every right to decide where the observer sits while you teach your lesson. Make it perfectly clear to them where you wish them to be by setting a chair somewhere at the back of the room with your lesson plan and a copy of your resources on it. It is absolutely guaranteed that they will speak to pupils about their work so make sure that you place them next to a pupil who is pleasant and positive, who will not be obtuse when you give instructions and whose work is marked up to date.

Lay the table. Set everything that you need out on a separate desk, in the order you will use them. Make sure this is somewhere inaccessible to pupils.

Be cool. Eat some breakfast and don't drink too much coffee – no one likes smelly teacher-breath ...

Expect the unexpected

So what happens if you've planned everything down to the last perfectly curled chest hair and then something (or someone) pops up to throw a spanner in the works? The following is a list of unpleasant experiences that befell teachers we have spoken to about their observation experiences. Prepare for them, learn from them, or simply laugh at the poor souls and be glad it wasn't you . . .

What do you do if . . . the observer doesn't turn up?

This is the cardinal sin of observers, and, apparently, a common one! L.J. Sweetness had spent two weeks fretting about the headteacher coming in to watch her lesson. Beginning her lesson weak through lack of food and sleep and still in a slightly befuddled daze from the medicinal vodkas the night before, she soon realized that her busy manager was clearly not going to turn up and had completely forgotten about the arrangement. So all you observers out there who are guilty of this unforgivable act of insensitivity, we would like you now to spank yourselves quite forcefully and promise to double-check your diary every morning from now on. Alternatively, you may need to consider getting yourself a new secretary.

To all you teachers, if this ever happens to you, we suggest that you send a pupil as soon as possible to establish whether the plonker intends to turn up at all. If they don't come rushing apologetically to your classroom, scrap your pimped-to-perfection lesson and jolly well save it for when they do decide to actually turn up.

What do you do if . . . the kids are intimidated by the observer?

Rick Studman-Suede was observed by his QA manager, Mr Bagley, who was also the deputy head in charge of pupil behaviour. Every pupil in the school was terrified of Mr Bagley, especially Rick's top set, immaculately behaved Year 7 class. Having planned a wonderfully interactive, exciting lesson involving whole-class discussion and role play, Rick's entire class sat silent and rigid in their seats, white-faced and wide-eyed, while Rick pleaded desperately, 'I'm sure *someone* would like to volunteer . . .?'

If this happens to you, there are two things you can do. The first and easier of the two is to use the pupils whom you know to be the most able as a resource. You know the ones – those little angels who will always know the answer and who are eternally seeking your approval. Make as if you are selecting pupils arbitrarily and we hope, for your sake, you have more than one in the class ...

A more difficult but more effective way to re-establish the classroom as a safe and relaxed environment, despite the presence of the school Rottweiler, is to involve the observer in your questioning and draw them into the lesson. Questions like, 'I bet even Mr Bagley didn't know that – did you, Mr Bagley?!' or 'Has that ever happened to you, Mr Bagley?' might come in useful here.

What do you do if ... there is a technical breakdown?

Well, always, always check equipment first. Video/DVD, television, OHP, computers – whatever it is, make sure that it is working and available before your lesson. J. Dogg Fresh, a member of the senior leadership team, was being observed by an Ofsted Inspector and was extremely nervous. After conducting the starter activity in his usual classroom, he marched the pupils and the inspector over to the lecture theatre to show them some slides. When they arrived, there was no screen to display the images (it had been borrowed by another anxious teacher to hide an untidy wall display). Flustered and sweating, J. Dogg trailed the kids and the enigmatically smiling inspector back to the classroom and proceeded to describe to the flummoxed pupils what they would have seen had the equipment been available. He then flopped dejectedly onto his chair and asked them to write about it.

The lesson to be learned here is always to have a plan B if you are using technical equipment. (Or maybe it should be simply to avoid using technical equipment where possible when you are being observed ...?)

What happens if ... your mobile phone goes off during the lesson?

Oh come on! Do we really need to tell you what our advice is here? This happened to Treacle T. Toner, who incidentally said NO ONE EVER rings her on her mobile! She had calmly questioned four likely culprits about the ringing before one of them said, 'Miss, I think it's coming from your bag . . .' Treacle T., utterly devastated, resisted the temptation to say 'Excuse me – I need to take this . . .' and disappear out of the room, never to be seen again. And fortunately too, because her observer, who had a great sense of humour, found it all extremely entertaining! It turned out to be a wrong number.

By the way – turn it off!

What happens if ... I'm subjected to a post-lesson grilling?

Some observers, especially the less confident ones, refrain from assigning a grade to your teaching before they have spoken to you and ascertained how you feel the lesson went. Often they are afraid of announcing an all-important number in case it comes as a total shock to you or else you perceive them as ridiculously generous. These are the observers who hang about at the end of your lesson, uttering benign phrases like 'I really enjoyed that!' or 'There are some real characters in that class, aren't there!'.

Assuming that your lesson went typically well, seize your advantage by conveying a sense of utter ease and contentment with all that has come to pass over the last hour or so. Avoid any worried expressions or anxious twitching that would allow a nervous observer to feel justified in leaning more towards 'Good' than 'Outstanding', just to be safe.

On the other hand, you might be faced with one of those more sadistic observers who appear to make the quality of your own evaluation of the lesson count towards your final assessment grade. This happens most often after interview lessons when the school wishes to establish how aware you are of your own strengths and weaknesses.

Never fear! In Table 2.3 below, we have provided a list of the five questions that your observer is most likely to ask you, once your pulse has returned to its normal resting rate and you *thought* it was all over. Consider them carefully now, close your eyes and imagine yourself giving the answers you would like to be able to give after a thoroughly outstanding lesson. Apparently the technique worked for Sven-Göran Eriksson . . . .

Table 2.3

What the observer might ask	What the observer should be thinking already
1. How well do you feel the introduction/starter activity went?	There was a prompt start to the lesson. You recapped on prior learning. You shared clear objectives with the pupils. Pupils were interested and they knew what to do.
2. How effective do you think your questioning of the pupils was?	Questioning was probing, challenging and was appropriate to the spectrum of abilities.
3. How well do you feel the pupils performed in the lesson? How much do you think they learned?	The pupils remained focused and on task. They had opportunities to develop as independent learners. They showed initiative, perseverance and enthusiasm. They were able to articulate what they had learned.
4. What aspect of your lesson did you feel went particularly well?	Everything! The strategies for differentiation were effective. The pace was good and the tasks were interesting, varied and well received by the pupils. ICT/numeracy/literacy was supported. There was a social/moral/cultural/spiritual aspect to the lesson. Teacher–pupil relationship was positive. Exciting AfL techniques were used. Etc., etc., etc.
5. Was there anything you would like to have changed about your lesson? Were there any missed opportunities?	Nope.

Trash it!

As mentioned in Chapter 1 (you didn't skip that, did you?!) we are providing you with some classroom transgressions to avoid when planning your pimped lesson. Read on and you'll see what we mean ...

Winging it

It's one thing to avoid over-planning your lesson for fear of losing that appealing air of spontaneity, but if you leave too much to chance, it is very unlikely that you will be able to tick enough of the 'Outstanding' boxes on the day to gain top marks overall. It is harder now than it ever has been to fulfil all the criteria necessary to make even the most generous observer feel confident about sticking their neck out and giving you an 'Outstanding'.

Last-minute photocopying

Well, you just know it's going to break down, chew up your originals and cover you in toner – don't you? Subsequently, all those amusing little cartoons and quotes that people have stuck up around the machine don't seem quite so funny anymore, do they ...?

Becoming the Devil Teacher from Hell in the preceding lessons

Have you ever noticed how as soon as your school learns that Ofsted are coming, you can hear twice the amount of stressed-out shouting emanating from classrooms and echoing down the corridors? And then you get people in the staffroom remarking on how the pupils' behaviour has suddenly taken a turn for the worse: 'It's typical, isn't it – they're usually a delightful class and now they suddenly start behaving badly, just when Ofsted is about to arrive.' We like to call this PISS – Pre-Inspection Strictness Syndrome. The symptoms are hard to recognize in yourself, because you are often totally unaware that your anxiety levels are causing you to behave differently with your class. Pupils are little barometers for your stress levels, and are surprisingly sensitive to changes in your manner. Consequently, if you appear uncharacteristically ruffled when they don't enter the room in a perfect, orderly line, your pupils become unsettled and behave atypically.

3

Pimp Your . . . Lesson Plan

> I have a cunning plan ...
>
> Baldrick, *Blackadder*

Stop gritting your teeth. Mop the sweat from your brow. Save the last fingernail you have not yet chewed for the day of your actual observation. Putting together the lesson plan itself can often be the most harrowing part of preparing for O-Day. It is here where you must articulate all your ideas, highlight all your successes and boast your ingenious application of all those pieces that form the masterpiece that is Your Lesson. It is also where you must elucidate all those little grey areas you told yourself you would think about later. Well, get out the INSET booklet that you jotted down all your ideas on and let's get pimping ...

There are a number of reasons why you need to put considerable time and effort into your lesson plan:

1. **The Maybelline factor.** You never see plain, disfigured or even downright homely girls in Maybelline advertisements and the reason is that (sadly) their make-up would not sell if the women buying it, in some small way, did not believe that it would get them that little bit closer to looking like Christy Turlington or Sarah Michelle Gellar. Your lesson plan is the same; sod the whole 'can't judge a book by its cover' thing, because your planning will be judged by what your observer sees on the carefully typed page you present to them.

2. **The *Extras* factor.** Andy Millman, played by the ever-hilarious Ricky Gervais in the BBC's comedy *Extras*, sees himself not as a mere 'extra', but as a 'background artist'. He, just like you, acknowledges that there is a lot more than meets the eye when it comes to show business and that all that background stuff, namely HIS role, is equally important to the overall product. Our stage is slightly less stylish: a garishly decorated classroom, rather than the television screen, but the principle is sound nonetheless. Prior learning, routines, unspoken methods of assessment and differentiation will all go under the radar if you do not explicitly point them out. The lesson plan is the ideal vehicle

for this, since it would be weird to provide commentary in a lesson.

3. **The Poirot factor.** Whether it is evidence for completion of your PGCE or NQT portfolio, your AST assessment performance management, or threshold assessment, there are crucial times when you need to be able to prove, with concrete evidence, that you are brilliant. Poirot never conjured up solutions to his cases from thin air; he relied on the evidence to support his instinct. Sadly, you must do the same. Detailed lesson plans, with observation reports to support them, are the perfect way to prove a number of aptitudes, experiences and skills.

When it comes to crafting the perfect lesson plan, there is no hard and fast answer to what must be included and what should be excluded. Our stance is 'the more the merrier'. This is, after all, the concrete evidence of what you have accomplished (hopefully!) during the lesson. You will have to adapt your lesson plan to fit the format and expectations of your school or department in terms of lesson planning, though we think that once they take a look at our pimped planning style, there'll be no looking back!

Sheika B. Ice was trying to keep her cool visage when the buzz spread through the school like head lice in a Year 2 class that those prophets of doom, Ofsted, would be darkening their door in only three working days. The last time the school was inspected, the English Department did not fare very well. The structure of English lessons was criticized and there were gaps in areas like 'moral, cultural, spiritual' and numeracy. Concerns were also expressed about the disparity between the results of girls and boys at both SATs and GCSE levels. While the rest of the department lamented that there was simply no way to get MATHS into an ENGLISH lesson, and that the boys in their catchment area were simply beyond help, Sheika knew what she had to do. She began to sort out her planning,

so that when those inspectors took one look at her lesson plan they would see that the only gaps in sight would be the gaping mouths of her colleagues as they marvelled at her 'Outstanding' assessment.

Though it sounds a bit like a recovery programme, we have identified 11 easy steps to help Sheika create the perfect lesson plan ...

Eleven easy steps to the perfect lesson plan

1. Provide background data for your class and the lesson

Your observer needs to know what sort of class you are teaching in order to make an assessment about whether you have pitched the lesson correctly and to understand how your lesson fits into the grand scheme of things. Be sure to make clear:

- how many students there are in the class, including the number of boys and the number of girls;
- the number of students on the SEN register and the number of statemented students, if applicable;
- how the lesson fits in to departmental schemes of work;
- the prior learning that has taken place in preparation for the lesson;
- the range of attainment levels in the class;
- whether the class is mixed ability or taught in sets.

2. Stipulate the main lesson objective that you will share with the class

The lesson objective you share with your pupils is not a description of the tasks they will complete during the lesson, but should be a reflection of what they will have achieved by the end of it. Here are some stems the DfES has identified (2002) in *Training material for foundation subjects* (www.standards.dfes.gov.uk) to help write effective lesson objectives:

- **To know that ...** This is for lessons where your aim is to share factual information, such as information about and the names of places, people, equipment, symbols, formulae, etc.
- **To develop/be able to ...** This type of objective would be used in a lesson where skills are being developed and techniques, analysis of information and knowledge are being used for a purpose.
- **To understand how/why ...** This targets understanding of concepts, reasons, effects, principles, processes, etc.
- **To develop/be aware of ...** This is used where your lesson focuses on expressing values and attitudes such as empathy, caring, sensitivity towards social ideas, feelings, moral issues, etc.

3. Detailing the learning outcomes

Demonstrating that you know what you intend your students to achieve during the lesson is as important as setting a clear lesson objective. You obviously need to know how they will arrive at the lesson objective, and this process, as mentioned earlier, is not always wholly visible. Your learning outcomes should describe not only the oral and written product, but also the quality and quantity you expect. Here you should identify skills that will be used to achieve the outcomes and prior learning, as well as the knowledge they will use to complete the tasks set. To put it as plainly as possible, the learning outcomes express what pupils will *do* or *produce*, such as discuss a concept, produce an essay or deliver a speech. The learning objective, by contrast, dictates the *skill* or greater *understanding* the pupils have acquired by the time they walk out the door.

4. Social, Moral, Cultural, Spiritual (SMCS) and Every Child Matters (ECM)

As mentioned in Chapters 5 and 6, it is acceptable that not every lesson you teach will have SMCS or ECM undertones. You should, however, be able to include one of these five features in your lesson somewhere, or be able to indicate how it is incorporated in the bigger picture. Just as spellings are not the sole responsibility of the English Department, and anything with a number does not need to be left to the mathematicians, SMCS must not be left to RE teachers alone. Do not allow yourself to fall into the trap of it 'not being your subject'. Check out Chapter 5 for some top tips on planning for and including these features in your lesson.

5. Literacy, numeracy and ICT

OK, broken record time. Elements of literacy and numeracy are not necessarily going to appear in every lesson, every time, but you should, without a doubt, incorporate elements of at least one of the two. Please consult Chapters 8 and 9 for further advice concerning these pertinent and mandatory elements of your pimped lesson.

6. Differentiation

You should ensure you use this section to list as many forms of differentiation as you possibly can; no lesson plan should be considered complete without at least five differentiation strategies. Name specific students you make allowances for; detail specific reasons why you have chosen or designed the resources for your lesson; justify your seating plan; name strategies you use to target dyslexia, reluctant readers, students with poor or exceptional literacy, behaviour, verrucas, bad breath; the long and short of it is that you must mention any and all allowances and provisions you make for your class just because they are who they are. By the by ... we hope you picked up on the little trick we included in there to catch those of you who weren't skim reading effectively ...

7. Assessment for Learning

This is another section which should boast a huge range of AfL wonders used in your 60 minutes of glory. No matter how trivial it sounds, be sure to articulate any and every way that you are evaluating the responses, reactions and understanding of the information and tasks that you are providing. By the same token, read through Chapter 4 to ensure that you have a crystal clear idea of the huge range of classroom goings-on that fall under the umbrella of AfL.

8. Resources required

This is the part of your lesson plan that is akin to a recipe. Here you get to make a list of the innovative and wonderful materials you are implementing to create your masterpiece. Be sure to list any books and materials that you have sourced and are using. This section, unlike the two previous, does not require you to list any- and everything ... do not feel obliged to list any of the following items that might be vital to your lesson:

- walls, windows and ceiling to protect students from the elements;
- two paracetamol because this class always gives you a headache;
- desks to hide under in the unlikely event of an earthquake;
- extra-strength anti-perspirant because you sweat under pressure;
- incontinence pants in case of a sudden, and unfortunate, attack of nerves.
- We think you get the idea ...

9. Lesson content

The meat and potatoes of your lesson plan. Lovely. In this portion of the lesson plan you need to describe, in a succinct and clear fashion, the planned events of your lesson, and separate them into convenient, easy to swallow sections. Not only should you break your lesson down into the obvious categories of starter, introduction, main activity and plenary (God Bless the National Strategy!), but also, within each of these headings, you should identify approximate timings, what the teacher is doing at each interval and what the students are expected to be doing.

10. Homework and links to subsequent learning

Homework is not always necessary; obviously, you only need to set it in accordance with your school's homework policy. It is, however, a good idea to make mention of any homework projects that will arise as a result of the lesson, or any that provided background in the lead-up to it. You should also mention briefly what lessons will take place in the wake of the lesson, to make clear how it all fits in to your long-term plan.

11. Long-term assessment strategies

You should provide some brief details about how the work done in the lesson will be assessed after the bell rings, and of how the activities and learning will build up to cumulative assessment in the future.

It is all well and good to talk about the important elements of an outstanding lesson plan, but to really put the theory into practice, a concrete example is necessary. Hold on to your seats ... here it is ... Ms Ice's lesson plan!!!

TEACHER: Sheika B. Ice	SUBJECT: English
CLASS/YEAR: 11	SET: 5 OF 7
DATE: Wednesday 24 January 2007	PERIOD: 2
NUMBER OF PUPILS ON REGISTER: 24	BOYS: 14 GIRLS: 8

CLASS BACKGROUND:
This is a relatively low-attaining class, with Yellis targets ranging from C to E and current attainment levels ranging from D to F. Poor attendance is an issue for four students in the class. Three of these attend work experience two days a week, resulting in three missed English lessons a fortnight. The fourth has long-standing health problems which keep her from school. Two students in the class are statemented: J. Barnes for dyslexia and T. Foster for behaviour. Nine others are on the SEN register for a range of challenges such as literacy, mild dyslexia, numeracy and ADHD.

LINK TO PREVIOUS LESSON AND PREVIOUS LEARNING:
Pupils have been studying the set poems that they must write about in their GCSE exam. This will be the fourth poem they have encountered by the set poet, Carol Ann Duffy.

LEARNING OBJECTIVE TO BE SHARED WITH PUPILS:
To develop an awareness of the moral issues and the ways they are presented in Carol Ann Duffy's poem 'Salome'.

LEARNING OUTCOMES – BY THE END OF THE LESSON PUPILS WILL:

- have understood the poem and considered the motives of the speaker;
- have used inference, deduction and empathy when responding to the character in the poem;
- have explored and evaluated the ways meaning, ideas and feelings are conveyed through the language and structure of the poem;
- have considered how poetic techniques such as rhythm, alliteration, imagery, etc. can contribute to the overall meaning of the poem;
- have considered alternative interpretations;
- have made contributions that take account of and build on other pupils' views;
- have responded to the poem critically, sensitively and in detail;
- have conveyed their responses in an appropriate way, using textual evidence.

SOCIAL/MORAL/CULTURAL/SPIRITUAL/CITIZENSHIP:
Class will consider the consequences of promiscuity and judge the motives of the characters in the poem.
Today's society will be discussed, with reference to *Celebrity Big Brother.*
The question will also be raised of whether there can ever be a valid excuse for certain behaviours.

NUMERACY:
Examination of the rhythm in the poem involves identifying discrepancies in the number of beats or syllables.

RAISING BOYS' ACHIEVEMENT:
Pupils seated boy/girl where possible to maximize performance. Active, kinesthetic activities. Paired task presented as 'Mission Impossible'. Series of short tasks. Opportunities to explore understanding through discussion.

LINK TO NC PROGRAMMES OF STUDY OR SYLLABUS:
Paper 2 of the English GCSE requires pupils to write about specific poems by Carol Ann Duffy and Simon Armitage and to compare them with a selection of pre-1914 poems.

STRATEGIES FOR DIFFERENTIATION:
- Series of short tasks to aid those pupils with shorter concentration spans.
- 'Missions' in envelopes differ in complexity and will be distributed according to ability.
- Each 'mission' allows for a basic personal response from less able pupils and an original and analytical response from the most able.
- Short interactive session to start the lesson and help pupils to focus.
- Paired work to ensure peer support.
- Teacher to circulate during paired work, offering help and guidance where most needed and stretching the most able.
- Tips provided on worksheets to help less confident pupils.
- Resources designed with large font to cater for J. Barnes' IEP.
- Seating plan is in place to allow for peer support. T. Foster to be sat independently at the back of the room unless working in a group or paired activity as per his IEP.
- The Pass-the-Parcel plenary ensures that even the least confident pupils are encouraged to contribute in a fun and non-threatening way.

ASSESSMENT FOR LEARNING:

- Seating plan to aid peer support and learning opportunities.
- Main lesson objective made clear on board.
- Interactive plenary to check and recap on learning.
- Homework requires pupils to 'teach' this poem to a parent/carer/friend/teacher.

STRATEGIES THAT WILL BE USED *DURING THE LESSON* TO ASSESS PUPILS' KNOWLEDGE, SKILLS AND PROGRESS:

- Teacher questioning to draw out and assess understanding.
- Students' oral contributions.
- Teacher circulates during individual work.

RESOURCES REQUIRED:

- Photocopies of the poem so that pupils can annotate it for their revision.
- Missions in envelopes.
- Pass-the-Parcel for plenary.

LESSON CONTENT (to include approximate timing):

Teacher activity	Pupil activity	Time (approx.)
INTERACTIVE STARTER ACTIVITY: Teacher introduces themes of poem and organizes relevant Uninvited Guests activity (pupils are familiar with this).	Volunteers play roles relevant to today's poem. Remaining pupils act as an audience to consider the behaviour of the characters.	10 minutes
WHOLE-CLASS ACTIVITY: Teacher reads poem and facilitates a discussion on promiscuity and self-respect and helps pupils to articulate their feelings about the main character in the poem.	Pupils give an initial response to the poem, sharing their thoughts on the meaning and their attitude towards the poet's persona.	20 minutes

Teacher questions pupils about specific poetic techniques to draw out understanding.	Pupils refer to specific sections or words to support their ideas. They consider Duffy's use of language.	
PAIR-WORK: Teacher gives each pair a mission in an envelope. Each mission is different and requires the pairs to give a personal response to the poem (see examples attached). Teacher circulates to offer guidance and facilitate learning through questioning.	Working in pairs, pupils use the information provided in their mission envelope, and attempt to provide a useful response to their task, which they can share with the rest of the class.	10 minutes
Teacher helps selected pairs to share their ideas with the class.	Pupils evaluate each other's work in a positive way, revealing what they have learned this lesson.	10 minutes
PLENARY: Teacher introduces Question-Filled Pass-the-Parcel. Teacher helps pupils to articulate their response to the question discovered in each layer. Questions will draw out what has been learned this lesson. Particular pupils can be targeted.	Pupils pass the parcel, stopping at intervals to unwrap a layer. As they discover their question, they must use what they have learned this lesson to answer it. They should refer to textual detail in the poem to support their answers.	10 minutes

HOMEWORK:
Pupils must 'teach' this poem to a parent/carer/friend/teacher and ask them to fill in the evaluation sheet (see attached).

BRIEF DETAILS OF NEXT LESSON:
Pupils will consider a fifth poem by Carol Ann Duffy and explore connections between it and previous poems studied.

HOW LEARNING WILL BE EVALUATED IN THE LONG TERM:
The evaluation homework sheet will be used to assess how well the pupils explained the poem.
Pupils' understanding will be evident in future essays about the poems of the set exam poets.

As you can see, Sheika has developed a thorough and clear account of exactly what she expects to occur in her lesson AND all the things most observers probably wouldn't see unless it is rubbed in their face. To remedy the concerns expressed about the attainment of boys in English from the last inspection, Sheika has included an additional section to her lesson plan, detailing how she has planned to target and differentiate for the boys in her class.

Trash it!

Sheika hit the nail on the head with this plan, but to ensure that you don't miss and end up with a thumb four times its natural size, be sure to avoid these errors:

- **Handwritten lesson plans.** You might be more comfortable writing things out by hand and may very well do your best thinking when using a pen rather than a keyboard. Even if this is the case, we must, at this point, invite you to join the rest of us in the twenty-first century and implore you to get those brilliant ideas word-processed after you have laid them all out. A typed-up lesson plan is always easier to read and follow, and presents a more polished, well-presented piece of work.
- **One side of A4.** If you are to follow our 11-step programme to success, there is NO way you will fit all your pimpfulness on one lousy side of A4, unless you shrink it down to a 6pt font. Since no one can *read* a 6pt font, and we know that you have much more to say than one side of A4 can hold, splash out on that extra sheet to make sure you really show off your stuff. If it's wasting trees you are concerned about, make sure you recycle BOTH sheets directly after the lesson.

Now that you've seen the light and are ready to dig the crumpled INSET booklet you used for brainstorming out of your pocket, it's time to get on with your lesson plan. Take a leaf from Sheika's little black book and make sure your lesson plan lands you in pimping prominence rather than 'Satisfactory' obscurity.

4

Pimp Your ...
Assessment for
Learning

Example isn't another way to teach, it is the only way to teach.

Albert Einstein

Before we dismiss Assessment for Learning as another 'initiative of the month', we must see it for what it is: the basic tenets of effective assessment. Although none of us cares for the thought of having to go through all of our schemes of work and add in another little column which explicitly states how we plan to incorporate AfL into the unit of work, it is not an unreasonable thing to be asked to consider. How are you discerning what the students have learned from your lesson and how are you sharing it with them? How are *they* discerning what they have learned and establishing how to improve? As much as we would all like to be able to justify our assessment of our students by saying 'Because I'm their teacher and I say so', this simply won't cut it when the proverbial inspector calls.

What we also must keep in mind is that (thank goodness!) AfL is so much more than just peer assessment and reading each other's work. The hairs on the back of our necks stand up and we break out into a cold sweat at the mere prospect of enduring the painful process of peer assessment on a daily basis. Believe it or not, you can make it fun, you can make it interesting, and you can make it look absolutely BRILLIANT for your lesson observation.

The QCA website (www.qca.org.uk) outlines 'The 10 Principles' of AfL, and though this makes it sound like AfL is a religious cult, it actually breaks down the major aspects of AfL that your observer will be looking for into easy to digest and implement pieces. Here are a few of the 'biggies' in terms of observation.

Principles of AfL

Principle 1: Ritual sacrifice of students to the assessment gods will bring about excellent GCSE results

Kidding. If only it were that easy.

Principle 1: Assessment for Learning should be part of effective planning of teaching and learning

When being observed, especially if the focus of the observation is how you implement AfL in your lessons, it is VITAL that you flag up in your lesson plan every means of assessment that you use in your lesson. Identifying numerous techniques in your lesson plan highlights what the observer should look for AND demonstrates your understanding of the wide net that is AfL.

Principle 3: Assessment for Learning should be recognized as central to classroom practice

Sadly, it won't bring about the best results if you spring these fabulous AfL techniques on your students for the first time during your observation lesson. We all know that students are usually suspicious of new things and often don't get it quite right the first time. In the few lessons leading up to your observation be sure to test your techniques of choice to ensure that your students understand what they are doing and that they are able to do it effectively. Being able to show (and flag up in your lesson plan, obviously!) that AfL is a part of classroom routine, rather than just a bit of one-off bling for an observation lesson, will definitely get you some Brownie points.

Principle 7: Assessment for Learning should promote commitment to learning goals and a shared understanding of the criteria by which they are assessed

And this here is where it is just so much easier to say 'It's a level 5 because I'm the teacher and I say so'. In actual fact, this aspect of AfL is one of the simplest for you to include in your observation lesson. To achieve this, you must share your learning objective with your class in an explicit and pupil-friendly way. If you are generating your own resources, be sure to include some success criteria on the resource which students can refer to regularly. This will also be useful when it becomes time to mark the piece of work. It will be as simple as highlighting or drawing attention to aspects of the success criteria they have excelled at, need to improve or have just plain forgotten.

Principle 9: Assessment for Learning develops learners' capacity for self-assessment so that they can become reflective and self-managing

EXCELLENT! Does this mean that if we get AfL right, they will eventually teach themselves and we can just sit back and watch? If we get this right, they will be able to write their own reports? One of the central bugbears of Assessment for Learning can be self-assessment. We cannot expect the shining faces before us to consistently be able to make the fine distinction between a 'level 5a' and a 'level 5c', but we *can* expect them to evaluate their learning. The expectation of Assessment for Learning dictates that students should be aware of their goals and how they are being assessed, but not necessarily that they can do this as competently as their teachers. We have all experimented with students assessing their own work, and it often results in their placing themselves three levels higher than they actually are and setting themselves a target like 'Write neater next time' or 'Make it sound more good'. The key to effective self-assessment is to make it specific: be sure that the students KNOW what aspect you want them to assess/improve/set targets for. Establishing an overall level for a piece of work they have done using assessment criteria that even experienced teachers can have difficulty making heads or tails of, is a daunting and even unreasonable task for most students to undertake. In the context of observation, the best way your students can demonstrate for your observer that they understand what they are learning is to be able to locate it in their own work and, hopefully, begin to look for SPECIFIC ways to improve it.

Luckily for you, 'Success Sorting', 'Keyword Feedback' and 'Colour-Coded Compliments' are all simple strategies that you can use in your observation lesson that will make it clear that this is exactly how you approach assessment in your classroom.

Like a fine wine, Assessment for Learning techniques get better with age. Though some of these ideas are great ways of employing

'The 10 Principles' for one-off lessons, others are much better introduced a few lessons before and established as a 'routine'.

> **J. Dogg Fresh was an outstanding teacher. He knew it, his department head knew it and his headteacher knew it, which is exactly why they were going through the arduous process of qualifying him as an advanced skills teacher. Though J. Dogg's flashy grill and swank sense of style had gotten him places in the past, he knew that he would have to drum up a little somethin' special to add this diamond to his chain.**
>
> **With his portfolio brimming over with pimptabulous evidence of his macktastic ways, J. Dogg needed some evidence that he was an Ace of Assessment, Prince of Appraisal and a Master of Marking. In short, he needed his Assessment for Learning pimped.**

Here's a little somethin' that J. Dogg could mull over in preparing for his assessment-focused observation.

Two Stars and a Wish

This is a really quick, really simple technique that can be used to peer assess any piece of work. Quite simply, the students seek out two things to compliment their peer on (the stars) and one thing they think could be improved (the wish). One of the principles of AfL stresses the importance of learner motivation and creating opportunity for success and target-setting in the work the students undertake. This peer-assessment method is most effective when students are given some guidance about the nature of the comments they give; remind them what the lesson objective is and be sure to let them know what they are looking for in the piece of work. This can be done either in the form of verbal assessment, shared with the individual student or the class, or as a written evaluation on the piece of work itself. Your observer will be impressed that you are stressing the learning objective you have set out and giving the students the opportunity to take ownership of the skills they have collectively learned. Even better, this will not take up very much of the limited and valuable time that you have to show the observer how 'Outstanding' you are!

An extension of this technique is 'Secret Admirer'. As a twist, you assign each member of the class to someone else in secret. The admirer's task is (without admitting to it) to pay their 'admiree' a sincere compliment about their contribution to the project/oral presentation/group task in secret. These can be done as simply as writing on a scrap of paper submitted en masse and redistributing once everyone has completed theirs. AfL stresses that any assessment has an emotional impact; this technique offers a forum for everyone to receive a compliment about something positive that they have been observed doing in class. Though students can be very reticent about saying nice things about people they are not 'bessie mates' with in front of a roomful of people, they are certainly more willing to be complimentary if they know they are not being judged by others on their remarks.

Yet another twist on this diverse strategy is 'Guess Who'. Here, you assign an admirer in the same fashion, but rather than secretly submit their positive observation, the pupils announce their statement, starting with the phrase, 'The person I was admiring did/made/said/showed/etc. . . .' and the class is left to guess who their admiree was.

Plenary Pals

This is definitely a technique that the students will have to be introduced to BEFORE the big observation. This technique involves choosing a pair/small group of students to take the responsibility of running the plenary session. You can do this effectively either on a rota basis, so the students know when it is their turn, or as a surprise on the day. The small group/pair is stopped about ten minutes before the plenary begins to give them time to prepare and to reflect on what the important keywords/ideas/concepts are and how they can draw these out of their peers. Especially when the technique is new to them, it is a good idea to give them some options on how to conduct their plenary. Perhaps they want to run a plenary game they are familiar with like 'Flyswatter' or 'Grandma's Trunk' (See Chapter 13); maybe they would like to host a quick quiz on what they have learned this lesson. They could also opt to prepare a series of flash cards and verbally summarize the main concepts. Be sure to remind the 'Plenary Pals' what the main objective of the lesson was and encourage them to link their plenary back to this. Your observer will be pleased to see you taking risks and releasing some control to your students, as this will demonstrate real confidence in your class and in your own teaching. Your observer will also be pleased to see your taking into consideration 'Principle 2', which stresses the importance of focusing on how students learn. We all know that the best testament of how well one understands something is being able to explain it clearly to someone else. Another noteworthy merit of this method is that it can quickly inform your planning by highlighting the ideas and concepts that may require clarification. If your lesson is a continuation of concepts learned the previous lesson, you could alter this slightly and have Starter Pals rather than Plenary Pals, and have a small group prepare the starter for your observation lesson, reviewing concepts previously learned.

Role Reversal

If you have a flair for the dramatic, both you and your students could have some fun with this technique! 'Role Reversal' involves the teacher taking on the role of a student who is not quite getting it right. It is the students' task to highlight where you are going wrong and what you can do to improve it. This is an excellent way to check sound understanding of a concept; if a student can tell you what should NOT happen, or, even better, how to improve or fix mistakes, they are developing assessment skills that should be able to cross over into their own work! The criticism provided by students acts as scaffolding for their peers and as a potentially funny illustration and a means of participating in the lesson. This technique lends itself especially well to oral or performance-based concepts, such as language orals, Speaking and Listening presentations in English, or performance techniques in drama. If you provide the students with some assessment criteria beforehand, students can also try their hand at grading or levelling your 'performance' as a means of shaping their criticism.

'Role Reversal' can also be used to consolidate non-performance concepts, and you can just talk through your work or ideas, be it method in preparing spaghetti Bolognese, balancing chemical equations or reviewing the components of the Earth's structure. An improved version of the infamous 'Traffic Light' system can be employed here: students can hold up a green card when they think you are getting it right, a yellow one when your performance or method could use some help and a red one when you are getting it all wrong. You can flag up certain moments in your 'performance' where you ask for the cards to be shown and for useful feedback; or you can wait until the end and debrief in its entirety.

Challenge the Parents!

This technique relies heavily on having parents who are supportive and students who are willing to approach their parents and include them in their schoolwork. This can be done as a whole-class homework assignment, but could possibly be more effective when used on a rota basis, where a group of 5–6 students complete the task at a time. For 'Challenge the Parents!' you provide your delegates with an outline for a task that both they and their parents must complete, pertaining to a recent concept or idea covered in class. This could take the form of a multiple choice quiz, a diagram to label, a paragraph/poem/ sketch/etc. that they must compose, completing a cloze exercise, testing them on some vocabulary or keywords ... the possibilities are endless. Inform the students that they must spend 5–10 minutes 'teaching' their parents about the concept, perhaps sharing notes made in their book, reading through a section of text together or visiting a specific website. The student and the parent both then complete the short task, and evaluate it together using a marking rubric provided by you. The student's challenge is to outperform their parent; a short defeat/victory comment from the parent would be a valuable add-on, as it is something the student can share with the class in their debrief.

This strategy is an excellent application of AfL principles as it provides both a teaching and an assessment opportunity for the students to work within, focusing on 'how they learn' (one of the ten principles outlined by QCA). Encouraging involvement from home is a positive feature as well, as parental encouragement and support can only motivate the students. This technique can be incorporated into your observation lesson in a variety of ways. You could use a portion of the lesson to design the task that the student and parent will undertake. If you choose to do this, you will obviously have to leave yourself some time to devise the marking rubric for the challenge, but your class will enjoy being able to take some ownership of the 'homework' that they will be setting for their parents. Selecting materials or compiling notes as a class that they think would be vital information to share with their parents in the 'teaching' portion of the task could also be an interesting feature of your lesson. This gives the class, as a whole, an opportunity to review and revise the concept, as well as providing a chance to model ways of presenting the information. Students debriefing their experience with their parents and sharing the defeat/victory comments could also be a means of incorporating this technique into the lesson. Having a class leader board to show how the students are faring against their parents would enhance the element of competition in the task.

Success Sorting

AfL stresses that students need to be motivated by targets and goals. They also need to be given the skills and criteria to allow them to maximize their potential and make the most of their learning opportunities by understanding WHAT they have to do in order to succeed. This strategy would be best used as part of an introduction to a cumulative project or activity that would focus on several acquired skills or bodies of knowledge. For 'Success Sorting', you need to make a series of cards or statements that have key features and skills which the pupils will need to exhibit in order to succeed on the project or assignment, as well as some cards detailing skills and features that would be distracting or erroneous. Students then need to 'sort' which belongs in each camp. This can be done with large cards where the whole class works together to sort the success criteria, as a paired task students do from their seats, or as a kinesthetic activity where the success criteria end up on one side of the room and the erroneous end up on the other. This activity will reinforce for your students exactly what you are looking for in their projects, and will reinforce for your observer that you convey clearly to your students what your expectations are.

Keyword Feedback

If you choose to incorporate peer assessment into your observation lesson the central tenet of such assessment must be practical advice on how to improve, as is clear from all of the literature and guidance surrounding AfL. Using 'Keyword Feedback' involves simply providing your students with words that they must use in their evaluation of their peers' work. When using peer evaluation, it is a good rule of thumb to give the students no more than two 'categories' to evaluate at one time. For example, if students are assessing each other's Shakespeare coursework in English, it would be wise to have them focus solely on the use of quotations and paragraphing. On a Key Stage 3 art project on cubism, you may wish to have students focus on the use of angles and range of colour. Once you have decided on the category(ies!) that you wish pupils to focus on, give your class a list of 3–5 keywords that must appear in their evaluation. If you are really organized (and skilled at pupil-speak learning objectives!), you could choose these keywords from learning objectives used in preceding formative lessons. Providing some sample statements of how to use the keywords in context would be a useful frame of reference for your class as well, and be an ideal way to show your observer your 'modelling' skills (no catwalk required). By choosing a limited range of features for your students to evaluate, you stand a much better chance of their providing each other with more useful feedback than 'I ♥ your drawing!'.

Colour-Coded Compliments

Let's be honest here ... What class have you ever had that does not LOVE to play with highlighters? Granted, this technique does require you to have a fairly extensive collection of the retina-offensive focal devices, but you can certainly improvise with coloured pencils or felt-tips. 'Colour-Coded Compliments' is not only a clever alliterative name for this peer-assessment technique, but also a means for students to identify sections of text that are outstanding, good or in need of a bit of help.

Each student (or pair of students) needs three colours to work with and a mutually agreed 'code' for what each represents. Ideally, these should be linked to specific features of the assignment (as mentioned in 'Keyword Feedback') and could be taken directly from the assignment outline or marks rubric. Quite simply, students highlight/circle/put a dot beside the features of the piece of work that they see meeting the criteria or fitting the comment. If students recognize that their classmate has failed to mention some key organs in their concept map on digestion, they may highlight this absence in the general area where it should be with a yellow dot. If they have gone over and above expectations by giving specific examples of enzymatic reactions that might take place in each area, this may warrant a purple dot. If they have mentioned 'the stomach' but have not gone into what actions occur there, perhaps this would warrant a green dot, requesting that they expand or add some more detail. Judgements passed can be as subjective or as objective as you like, so long as it is made clear to the class what specific features they are seeking out. This kind of structured peer assessment is perfect for an observation lesson as it allows you more control and predictable responses from your class at a time when surprises are the last thing you are looking for.

And, finally, some good old standbys ...

- Dig out some old exams, essays or exemplar work for students to assess or 'improve'. Don't forget to Tippex the name out ...
- Set a routine for students to copy the daily objective into their books at the top of their work. Be sure to make reference to it regularly in the lesson to remind them (and your observer!) of the purpose of the lesson.
- Provide assessment or success criteria for any significant piece of work the students undertake. These pointers can be formal, typed up on a writing frame or marking rubric, or informal and developed together as a series of bullet points on the board.
- Include a target-tracking or setting sheet in your students' exercise books or on the cover sheet of an assessment piece. If you can flag this up to your observer during the lesson, it is an excellent way to show that AfL is central to your regular practice.
- If the students' books have been recently marked (which they obviously will have been if you are being observed!), make a point of giving students some reflection time in the lesson to mull over your comments and make any corrections or alterations that are necessary.
- If you use a seating plan, draw this to the attention of your observer. Quite frequently this is also a means of facilitating AfL, as you have (presumably) organized it in a mutually beneficial fashion for peer assistance and learning opportunities.
- Be sure that your displays in the classroom contain exemplary student work and/or tools and techniques that students can refer to in order to improve their work.

When you are planning to show off your enviable understanding of Assessment for Learning, it is important to be aware that your observer is likely to speak to the pupils themselves in order to ascertain how well your assessment techniques are helping to enhance their attainment in your subject. In order for you to ensure that your pupils are well prepped in how to emphasize their teacher's brilliance when called upon, we have compiled a list of the five AFL-related questions inspectors most commonly ask of students during lesson observations:

1. Do you know what grade/level you are achieving at the moment?
2. Do you know what grade/level your teacher wants you to aim for?
3. Do you know what to do in order to improve your work?
4. How does what your teacher writes in your book, help you to understand how to improve your next piece of work?
5. What have you learned in this lesson that you did not know before?

The action to take, in the light of these common questions, is obvious:

1. Prior to the observation lesson, ensure that you have told every pupil what their current attainment level is. You may need to reiterate this quite firmly by writing it in the front of their books. Students can be a little dozy about this sort of thing – even if you have awarded the same grade for their last six pieces of homework.
2. Again, you need to highlight in their exercise books each pupil's target grade (even if they've just received this information on their school reports or you told them last night at Parents' Evening).
3. You will, of course, have written a target for improvement after each piece of work you have marked, but just in case they haven't actually read your comments (sound familiar?) you can ask pupils to copy out their target for improvement at the top of their next piece of work. A serious pimping device could be a laminated bookmark for each pupil, detailing their target and attainment grades, followed by a

brief statement explaining what aspect of their work they need to focus on. The laminating part of it isn't just to satisfy your craving for that heady, addictive smell of melting plastic; it also allows you to wipe the bookmarks clean when their attainment level changes or you need to give them a new target for improvement.

4. Make sure exercise books are marked carefully and handed back to pupils well before the lesson observation. A target should be written after each piece of work. 'V. good', 'Well-tried' or 'Neat work' just doesn't cut it anymore. Neither does a giant tick.

5. The infamous 'What have you learned this lesson?' question is the reason why an excellent plenary is so important. Check out Chapter 13 for some clever ways to guarantee that your pupils answer this question with enthusiasm and confidence.

Trash it!

When aiming to impress with your application of Assessment for Learning, here are some approaches that are all played out:

- **Unguided self-assessment.** From A* to G, students are not equipped with the experience or will to assess a piece of work (their own or a peer's) in a useful way without some guidance. So next time you go to tell your students 'Read through your partner's work and give them some useful comments', back that ass up and think about some clear guidelines!
- **Embarrassing displays of undeserved praise.** Let's face it, not all pieces of work are worthy of effusive praise. Telling a child that they have done an excellent job of underlining the title does not qualify as good assessment. It is embarrassing. Sometimes tough love is the only way forward, so find tactful ways of helping them improve their work, rather than hallucinating successes that aren't there.
- **Ridiculous reward tokens.** Rewarding students for a job

well done is imperative to effective assessment, but let's get serious: you have to give them something they actually care about. Be clear about this: laminating a piece of paper saying 'Well Done' does not make it an exciting reward.

Undoubtedly AfL is something that your observer will be keeping their beady little eyes out for, and the more concrete and explicit you can make your use of it, the better. Do not feel like you have to re-invent the wheel or begin doing things that feel unnatural or forced. Odds are that you have been 'Assessing for Learning' through your good practice without labelling it as such. The trick now is to drape it in velour, add some diamanté and impress your observer with your pimptastic ways . . .

> There is no moral precept that does not have something inconvenient about it.
>
> Denis Diderot

Isn't it annoying when non-teachers go on about the amount of holidays teachers get? You know the ones. They spend most of their working day sitting in quiet working atmospheres with polite adult company before going home to watch telly or maybe do a little light housework. No marking. No planning. No soul-searching self-evaluation. No beating themselves over the head with a stick for the little mistakes they made or worrying about that pupil's poem that could possibly have been a suicide note in disguise. Then, when you mention you're a teacher, they laugh heartily and say, 'Ah, yes, but you're in it for all those holidays you get, aren't you!'

Let's set the record straight right now for all the people who have ever said this or something similar: outstanding teachers do not get any more holiday time than any other profession. They have to mark pages and pages of essays, exams and projects; they have to plan months' worth of lessons; they have to design and produce resources; they have to write reports; they have to read government directives; they have to keep accurate records ... the list is endless. And, yes, all of that has to be done in their *spare* time – well, when did you think they did it? They're TEACHING the rest of the time, aren't they? You plonkers!

So if we're not in teaching for the holidays (and we're clearly not in it for the money!) why have we chosen such a demanding, intense occupation? The answer is simple: we clearly all want to make the world a better place. We want to mould the next generation into strong-minded, compassionate, independent and free-thinking individuals. And what is the best way to do that? Well, include a Social, Moral, Cultural, Spiritual (SMCS) objective into your lesson plan, of course!

Honey T. Slim was one of those 'save-the-world-one-pupil-at-a-time' believers, but she was stuck in the wrong school. At first sight, you might think it was a perfect job – no one ever checked up on her; in fact, she'd only been observed once in two years (and that was only for a period of 20 minutes because the SMT member had turned up late and left early). Perhaps it was because she was implicitly trusted to do a good job – but actually that didn't make her feel much better. You see, Honey felt that no one gave a tiny rat's bottom about whether she was an excellent teacher or an appalling one. To be honest, poor, sweet Honey just felt as if no one cared, full stop. So the job didn't bring out the best in her, and for the last few months, she had only been half-heartedly helping the human race, while spending the rest of the time feeding her need for acknowledgement and approval down at the local karaoke bar.

We tell you this, because when people – teachers or pupils – don't feel appreciated and cared for, after a while they don't work as hard. Can you see where we're going with this? Remembering to include a little moral, spiritual, cultural or social input in your lesson is part of what makes pupils feel valued and respected. We've all sat in those meetings where no one seems to give a damn about your opinion or, worse still, about your feelings. No one seems to place any value on what you may think, be it your beliefs, experiences or the questions you may have. You shut down and resign yourself to a boring two hours, or else inwardly you feel thwarted and begin to exhibit a sort of sulky resistance and exasperation.

Try to think of the SMCS element of your lesson in this way. For pupils, this layer of the lesson is the evidence that you care about them as people as well as caring about their grades. It is the fact that you don't sit them in silence, copying from the board, but allow them opportunities to discover, explore, negotiate, argue, listen, contemplate and socialize as well as learning about the wider world and seeing what they are learning in context.

Honey T. Slim applied for a post elsewhere and, desperate to change jobs, was particularly nervous when she attended the interview. As is traditional these days, the interview process involved teaching a lesson. Following the rules for pimping one's Preparation, Honey did a little research into the school and

59

learned that the new headteacher, who had recently been appointed, was currently ardently promoting the school as one which would 'turn out well-rounded citizens' as well as academics. She knew it was imperative, therefore, to exploit every opportunity for pimping the SMCS element of her interview lesson. It was time, once more, to turn back into Superteacher: saviour of the pupil race, Mr Miyagi in The Karate Kid, Michelle Pfeiffer in Dangerous Minds, Robin Williams in Dead Poets Society, Dumbledore in a shiny, leopard-skin suit.

Desperate times call for desperate pimping, and we suggested to Honey that she try to incorporate some of the following cross-curricular strategies for emphasizing the SMCS component of her teaching, into her interview lesson.

Teamwork

Any task that requires pupils to work together in order to achieve a shared goal is developing their social skills – yes, it really is as easy as that! To even begin to glimpse the giddy heights of 'Outstanding', your teaching must involve peer interaction in some way, whether it be through building on one another's ideas through whole-class discussion, or through a structured paired or small-group activity.

So how do we pimp the teamwork activities in our lessons? Well, the first thing to do is to directly share the Social Development objective with your pupils. Rather than saying, 'I'd like you to work in pairs to do this and I'll come round and help you . . .', give the pupils specific instructions about how they should work together. For example: 'I will be looking for people who are really listening to one another and taking each other's ideas into account. If you don't agree with something, be brave enough to explain why. If your partner is not contributing very much to the discussion, try to draw them in to the conversation by asking them questions in a polite, friendly way.' If your observer still hasn't picked up their pen to note something down about your guru-like qualities, you can always add, 'That way, kids, you'll be developing your social skills at the same time!'

If you have a really obtuse observer, you might wish to produce a resource to assist the teamwork activity in your lesson. A discussion frame would be ideal here. This could be anything from a simple list of points to consider, to precise instructions as to how the discussion should be conducted, or, for you complete control freaks out there, a series of sentence starters to really structure the pupils' talk. You may also wish to model the techniques necessary for a successful group or paired discussion. You could take a volunteer for this and then demonstrate to the class how to initiate a discussion, and explore ideas in a productive way. You might also include examples of how not to behave, by blocking a suggestion, missing opportunities to build on ideas or monopolizing the conversation. Pupils can then be invited to comment on the techniques you used and decide what moved the talk forwards and what did not. Check out 'Role Reversal' in Chapter 4 for further information on employing this strategy.

Encouraging personal opinion

Yes, of course this counts. See? And you thought the whole SMCS bit was going to be difficult! Obviously, any activity that requires pupils to formulate an opinion on a meaningful topic is equipping them with the experience they need to avoid becoming 'don't know, don't care' antisocial blobs.

In an observation lesson, it is important, therefore, to be seen to encourage and celebrate differences of opinion and belief. Make room for this in your lesson and accept all ideas without judgement – even the silly ones. However, be sure to pick up on any obvious prejudice or stereotyping.

Encouraging empathetic response

This is a nice easy one, and will naturally form a part of lessons in many subjects. It involves simply asking pupils to imagine how somebody else might feel or have felt; for example, a historical figure, a fictional character, someone from a different culture or country, etc., etc. The exercise could be an oral one or it might form part of a written exercise – the old 'writing a diary entry' trick, for example.

By doing this, you are giving your pupils an opportunity to exercise a very important life skill: the ability to put themselves in another's shoes. And, you never know, maybe – just maybe – they might be a tiny bit more understanding the next time you fail to look sufficiently delighted when they hand you their 20-page essays to mark the day before the half-term break.

Lessons in life

We are all aware that one of the most effective ways to engage a pupil's interest is to draw a link between what they are learning and their own popular culture. The growing trend in reality TV has sent a Mexican wave of interesting lessons through schools everywhere. The issues and controversy which always form such an integral part of these programmes conveniently seem to provide reference material for a plethora of topics covered by the curriculum. In relating the lesson's content to concepts within the pupils' own frame of reference, you are highlighting the link between what they are learning and their lives outside the classroom. This concept is at the heart of the spiritual, moral, cultural and social element of a lesson. We often, albeit unwillingly, make it far too easy for pupils to view what they learn in lessons as being useful only for passing exams. A decent observer will not fail to notice your willingness to combat this perception.

Plagiarism

This sounds like an odd one, but we include it as a ready-made pimping device for moral, spiritual, cultural and social emergencies across the curriculum. Plagiarism has implications for every subject and there are always opportunities for illicit copying, either from each other or from those infuriating websites with names like 'instanthomeworknow.com'. You can also draw clear links between this and other theft-related issues such as illegal downloading of music and films from the internet and shoplifting. Initiating a discussion about the moral implications of plagiarism is an ever-ready way to include SMCS as a clear but integrated part of your lesson plan.

Family homework

Setting homework which requires a pupil to converse in a meaningful way with a member of their family obviously serves to enhance their social development, particularly if traditionally they do little more than grunt 'Nothing much' in response to the ubiquitous 'What did you do at school today?' question, before sitting down in front of a computer game for four solid hours. Tasks like 'Get a parent or carer to test you' may allow the less diligent parents to escape their duties too easily. Instead, ask pupils to interview their parents about a relevant topic and record the parents' responses. Alternatively, ask your pupils to *teach* what they have learned to a parent or carer and, using an evaluation sheet provided by you, have the parents feed back to you how well they understand what they were *taught* (see Chapter 4).

Introducing moral dilemmas and hypothetical questions

This technique for developing SMCS awareness lends itself particularly well to starter activities but is definitely easier to use in some subjects than in others. You may recall hazy adolescent memories of games such as 'Truth or Dare' or 'Never Have I Ever ...' that use this principle. Applied in the classroom, learners are presented with a hypothetical situation which requires them to engage on a very personal level with the dilemma and explore their own moral stance. Most young adults will respond to the imagined situations with an immediate gut reaction, but their peers may be able to coax them to investigate their own feelings a little further.

To impress your observer with your slick, flip-of-the-wrist links between your subject-based focus and your stunning SMCS provision, these thought-provoking questions obviously need to be directly relevant to the lesson content itself. Fortunately, unless you are extremely unlucky, or you are forced to cover very tedious subject matter, it is likely that an opportunity for some sort of moral deliberation will reveal itself to you at some point while you are planning the lesson. If, however, during your observation lesson, a pupil spots a moral issue raised by the lesson topic, for example whether something should be permitted or not, just go with it. Children and young adults often have a very strong sense of justice and injustice. Just make sure that you reiterate the words moral, spiritual, cultural and social well within the observer's earshot!

Happy holidays!

Ofsted often turn up around Christmas time, don't they? *We* like to think that, contrary to popular belief, this is not because they worship the Antichrist, but rather it is to kindly provide us with a very easy way to incorporate a spiritual or cultural element into our lessons. By wangling a little bit of Christmas into your teaching, you are quickly and effectively ticking that SMCS box and spreading a little festive cheer while you're at it. If it's just too early for Santa, there is bound to be some other religious or cultural celebration coming up that you could bring somehow into your lesson. However, we've said it before and we'll say it again: Don't hand out Easter wordsearches; don't hand out wordsearches with pictures of Easter on them; in fact, don't hand out wordsearches at all. Bad, *bad* wordsearches.

6

Pimp Your ...
Every Child
Matters

> The future of the world is in my classroom today, a future with the potential for good or bad ... Several future presidents are learning from me today; so are the great writers of the next decades, and so are all the so-called ordinary people who will make the decisions in a democracy. I must never forget these same young people could be the thieves and murderers of the future. Only a teacher? Thank God I have a calling to the greatest profession of all! I must be vigilant every day, lest I lose one fragile opportunity to improve tomorrow.
>
> Ivan Welton Fitzwater

Every Child Matters. Teachers have, of course, been aware of this for centuries; it is the rest of the country who have only just caught up. For people who have devoted their working life to the education of young people, Every Child Mattered long before the idea was presented to Parliament by command of Her Majesty in September 2003. The trick now, however, is to make a concept which has hitherto been a natural, integrated part of our teaching, appear as a revolutionary, newfangled bit of bling that leads directly to one of the following five outcomes:

1. Being healthy
2. Staying safe
3. Enjoying and achieving
4. Making a positive contribution
5. Achieving economic well-being.

Let's tackle these one at a time ...

1. Being healthy

It's not easy to use your one-hour lesson to promote the benefits of a healthy lifestyle to a burger-eating, gum-chewing, inactive teenager, especially when you are trying to simultaneously ensure a hundred other things, including that the pupils actually learn the relevant information required to pass their exams. We would like to offer the following way to cater for this strand of ECM.

Some teachers like to begin their lessons with a sort of quirky, kinesthetic activity. These are exercises which do not directly relate to the lesson, but which prime the brain to be more receptive to learning in general. OK, so you're not going to make a significant difference to the neurological make-up of each kid in a few five-minute sessions, but the sentiment is there and an observer will definitely appreciate your valiant efforts to combat the insidious brain inertia that can infect the teenage generation. This sort of 'brain sport' is essentially any physical activity which requires the brain to focus in order to complete the task successfully. Do you remember the first time someone challenged you to pat your head while rubbing your tummy? It probably took you a little while before you stopped messing up your hair with a pat that looked suspiciously like a rub to everyone else. The following examples are suitable for use in any lesson, either as a starter, or as a concluding activity, or to provide a much-needed break from intense work at an appropriate point in the learning.

Try the following widely used exercises yourself before you try them out on your pupils. You may find some of them more challenging than you would think.

Twofold

Fold your arms in the normal, instinctive way you would fold them. Easy enough. Now try folding them the opposite way. You may well find you need to think about this. Keep crossing them one way and then the other until each way feels equally comfortable.

Vicious Circles

With one arm, draw a circle in the air, moving outwards from your chest like a wheel. With the other arm, draw a circle that rotates inwards towards your body. Keep both wheels rotating in opposite directions at the same time. Tricky, huh? Once you've mastered the move, try to do it faster and faster without losing the motion.

Numbers Up

In the air, draw different numbers with each hand, simultaneously. For example, you could try to draw a number 3 with the left hand while attempting a 5 with the right. Keep practising until you can do it easily.

Brain Breathing

Stand up straight and stretch out your arms above you as if trying to reach something suspended from the ceiling. Breathe deeply. And relax!

Helping Hands

In the air, trace a particular word backwards using the hand that you do not typically use for writing. Now try tracing the word with both hands simultaneously; one hand moving from left to right, the other moving from right to left. You may wish to check your accuracy by attempting this with pens and paper.

There is nothing to stop you devising your own programme of kinesthetic activities to maximize brain power. You don't have to be a rocket scientist. If it's an action that you find difficult, but are eventually able to master, it will work for your pupils. Just don't practise them in a lit window with the curtains open. Your neighbours may begin to worry about your general sanity.

Crazy Counters

Finally, a good activity to ensure that all pupils are focused and concentrating is the counting game. To do this, every pupil must put their heads down on the desks so that they cannot communicate with any of their classmates. Working as a team, the class must call out numbers in sequence, but only one pupil may speak at a time. If more than one pupil calls out the next number, the whole class must return to zero and start again. Typically, players are unable to get much further than number 5 before they realize that they all need to leave considerable pauses between each number in order to avoid calling out at the same time.

2. Staying safe

You could, of course, engineer a spectacular fight between pupils in your lesson and then charge in, cloak billowing, to wrestle the offenders apart and save the day (don't pretend you haven't had that fantasy at some point). This would definitely provide ample evidence for the observer of your heroic efforts to ensure that the kids *stay safe*. The downside to this cunning plan, however, is that a. you may find people catch on after your third or fourth observation lesson; and b. you may end up with a black eye.

Instead, do something far, far less exhausting: simply make it quite clear that you have assigned a supportive peer to each pupil, who can offer assistance and ideas during paired or group activities. This is something which will be commonplace for you anyway, as it simply involves instructing pupils whom they should work with. In this way we are teaching pupils to draw support from one another, to turn to one another for help and advice and to be readily available to assist others in need. Staying safe has never been so easy ...

3. Enjoying and achieving

We've pretty much got this one covered in every other chapter, which is why this is the easiest aspect of ECM to refer your observer to in your lesson plan. Simply draw attention to all the fun, exciting activities that you have built into your lesson. Gone are the days when an intimidating headteacher can walk past your open classroom door and frown at the laughter and frivolities emanating from within.

4. Making a positive contribution

Well, this one really is in the bag, isn't it? Take a look at the activities described in other chapters which are designed to encourage pupils to actively contribute to the lesson. You may wish to organize your tasks in such a way that obliges every pupil to contribute at least once. On the other hand, you could try concentrating on getting a particularly high-quality response out of a smaller number of pupils in this one particular lesson.

5. Achieving economic well-being

Really? So they're not asking for much, then? Teachers these days – tch! They have it so damn easy ... Actually, there is a very simple way to attend to this requirement: draw clear links in your lesson between the qualifications the pupils are preparing for and the jobs that these qualifications will open up for them. You could refer to the likely attitudes of potential employers in a casual way or even draw the pupils' attention to a classroom display, poster or list of the jobs that require a level of competence in your subject.

We would really not recommend that you attempt to cater for every one of these ECM outcomes in a single lesson. There's a difference between being an outstanding teacher and an insufferable boff. And you don't want to end up hated by all your colleagues; after all, every teacher matters too.

Trash it!

Preaching

A fellow colleague once revealed that when she was a pupil herself, her English teacher conveniently skipped the only interesting chapters of the D.H. Lawrence novel they were studying and talked to them about 'Sin' and 'Divine Retribution' instead. By the end of the course, even the once devout Christians had rebelled and were smoking behind the bike sheds on a regular basis. The truth is, once pupils know that you feel strongly about something, they often take the opposite stance on purpose, even if they like and admire you. You probably know adults who do this too. It doesn't make them bad people; they just derive an immense pleasure from debates and disagree in principle in order to provoke an intense discussion. No matter how passionately you feel about an issue, try to remain impartial and show the observer that you are allowing the pupils to explore and formulate their own ideas and opinions. Finally, it is also important to remember that it is unethical to use your position to pass on your own ideology to young people, whether it's religious, political or philosophical.

7

Pimp Your . . . Differentiation

My problems all started with my early education. I went to a school for mentally disturbed teachers.

Woody Allen

Once upon a time in a faraway land there was a classroom. Now this wasn't any ordinary classroom; it was a magic classroom with a magic doorway that made magic things happen to anyone that crossed its threshold. You see, this magic threshold made sure that, no matter what the discipline, no matter what the year group, no matter what the gender and no matter what the agreeable or disagreeable behaviour tendencies, all who crossed it were the same. All students in the magic classroom had the same reading age and the same numeracy skills. Emotional baggage and dislikes for ANY subject were forgotten and misconceptions were promptly amended. When Mr Flash E. Smooth, the Teacher-Prince that had been assigned to the magic classroom, discovered this, he ran for the hills, never to return to the magic classroom again.

Why, you ask, would Mr Smooth do such a foolish thing? Surely it would make lesson planning and delivery so much easier! The answer is simple:

It would be BORING.

Though we definitely wince (deepening those already pesky crow's-feet) at the mention of the word 'differentiation', it is not because we hate having different children in our classrooms; it is because of the images of extra work that we conjure up in our heads as a result of it. Let's not misunderstand the message of the magic doorway: there are certainly some students that we all wish were a little bit less different and there are DEFINITELY cases of emotional baggage and personality deficiencies that we would like to check at the door, but sadly, it ain't gonna happen.

Differentiation does not mean planning 26 different micro-lessons catered to each child's individual learning needs that you deliver in a preferred medium for 2.3 minutes each. It also does not mean redesigning worksheets for the five different levels of attainment you might have in your classroom. It's merely about making the lesson as accessible as possible to the 26 shining faces in front of you. YOU know them; you know what works for them and what doesn't.

We differentiate in our own lives all day, every day. At Christmas dinner, you know not to sit next to Uncle Jim because he, ahem, reacts poorly to stuffing, so you choose a seat that is more appropriate for your olfactory preferences. When you have rented a film you've been dying to see and know that sitting in the comfy corner of the sofa (you know what we're talking about, we all have one) will cause you to be asleep before the credits have rolled, you choose to sit in the armchair instead so you are sure that your £3.50 was not spent in vain. You know that if you go grocery shopping straight after school with a little rumble in your tummy you WILL end up spending roughly £75 more than you were intending, so you take an apple to eat before you go, or perhaps purchase a chocolate bar on the way in. Common sense, right? You are merely taking tasks that, through experience, you have learned carry their own little set of challenges with them, and adapt them so they work better for you. Classroom differentiation need be no different!

In Ofsted's *Good teaching, effective departments* (2002), good teachers are identified as ones who 'showed thorough knowledge of pupils as individual learners' and who plan lessons and schemes of work that are 'matched to the needs and interests of different pupils' (www.ofsted.gov.uk). Though that sounds daunting, it need not be. We tweak and twist past projects, alter our delivery style and even sometimes change the physical layout of our classroom to differentiate every day and every time we encounter a new group of individuals. Often this is done just to preserve our own sanity, and the educational benefits that ensue are merely collateral. If you've taught for two years or twenty-five years, it is near impossible to deliver the same lesson in an identical fashion. And who would want to look in their planner, see that it is 7 October and know that you must be teaching the lesson on introducing trigonometry? You even know that you will tell the joke about mathematicians at the beach ten minutes in. (*Q:* Why do you rarely find mathematicians spending time at the beach? *A:* Because they have sine and cosine to get a tan and don't need the sun!) Don't get it? Ask a maths teacher ...

When being observed, it is not so much that you try to weasel in wacky and innovative methods of differentiation; it's about showing that you know the class and have planned the lesson in a way that you know will elicit a positive response from your unique class.

Let's take a closer look at ways this can be done ...

Macktastic G. **Dazzle had been workin' his stuff in the same Music Department for seven years. His HoD, a crusty traditionalist who went to primary school with Chopin (or at least looked like he could have done) was observing him as a part of his annual performance management. Since he had arrived, Dazzle had been a 'good' teacher in every sense of the word ... he was well liked by the students, followed departmental and school protocol and schemes of work to the letter and had involved himself in many different extra-curricular projects to raise the profile of the Music Department. To add to this list of 'good' things, Dazzle had never managed to surpass a 'Good' rating on his annual observation.**

Not exactly dissatisfied with being 'Good', Macktastic still wanted to push himself this time and beat his old rap with an 'Outstanding' for this observation. Looking over his HoD's observation notes from last year, Macktastic noticed that an 'area for improvement' was the need to cater to a wider range of achievement in the lesson. 'Differentiation he wants, differentiation he will get,' thought Macktastic to himself as he sat down to plan his lesson. He was going to do anything it took to pimptazzle that lesson AND show exactly how diverse his teaching could be.

To get started, there are some things that we do to differentiate in a lesson that sometimes we don't even acknowledge as differentiation. It is very important to flag these up for your observer as they are not always visible, and your observer will not know you've even considered them unless you make it explicit.

- **Seating plans.** Never underestimate the power and effect of the seating plan. It ticks the differentiation box from so many different angles that it could make your gold tooth spin. The seating plan allows you to differentiate according to:
  - Behaviour. Nothing like splitting up 'Danielle' and 'Kayleigh' so they can't pass notes all lesson; or 'Jake' and 'Wayne' so they stop flicking small balls of paper into 'Danielle's' hair.
  - Academic ability. If you have tasks that are structured to specific attainment levels, you would no doubt want your students grouped so that they were collaborating with another student working on the same project as them.
  - Peer assistance. If your class is short on support staff (and whose classroom isn't?), you undoubtedly utilize (in the nicest sense of the word) high-attaining students to assist students that you know need that little bit of help. Through an unspoken, and often unwitting, agreement, these pairings are usually fruitful and keep both parties challenged and on task.
  - Gender. Especially for Key Stage 3 groups, it is sometimes mandatory to mix up the girls and the boys by force rather than by choice as they often will not work together without being directed to do so. This kind of pairing/grouping is a good way to add diversity to the ideas they generate.
  - Location in the classroom. For those students that have difficulty behaving or concentrating if they are more than six inches from the teacher it is important that you try to keep them near you. By contrast, you may wish to put poorly behaved pupils at the back of the room, so they do not have an audience to perform for. The moral of the story is that there is no hard and fast rule about where to place 'types' of students. We must give considered thought to how we organize our classrooms to maximize learning for all.
- **Using your starter as a recap.** Sounds like common sense, but your starter can be a key tool for your differentiation as it targets many students' differentiation needs. It targets the

forgetful ones who may need reminding of concepts covered or who were still foggy at the end of last lesson about how something worked. It also assists students with poor attendance that may have missed vital learning; though it obviously does not replace missed lessons, it at least provides some scaffolding and frame of reference. Recapping on prior learning also motivates reluctant or struggling learners as they start the lesson with success and something they are familiar with, rather than being bombarded with something new to absorb the second their bum hits the chair. Check out Chapter 12 for scintillating ideas on carrying out your starter.

- **Setting flexible tasks.** If you set a class a task which can elicit only one precise, correct response you have probably just walked into the 'magic classroom' mentioned at the beginning, or you have been given a freakishly homogeneous group whom you can expect to finish a given piece of work all at the precise same moment. If differentiating by outcome is the kind of differentiation you are going for, it is important to allow for some interpretation/experimentation/critical thinking within your tasks to ensure that your high flyers have a chance to stretch themselves and that those who are struggling to get off the ground will be able to achieve as well.
- **Providing examples/model material.** This gives struggling students something to aim for and higher achievers something to gauge their own work against. Classroom displays can be a great way to provide this support.
- **Teacher circulation.** An obvious one perhaps, but when 'working the room', you are creating an opportunity to stretch the more able and assist those who are struggling.

You are probably looking at the above points and thinking 'Yes, AND . . .' and 'I already do all those things', but this is the point: be sure to include your own explanation of how you apply these things in your lesson plan to ensure that your observer knows they are part of your differentiation strategy. Looking for something a little racier, a little more exciting? Try using some of the following tactics to shape your lesson.

Use popular culture

One of the greatest hurdles that we face is actually capturing the hearts and minds of our fickle audience. One method of attempting to scotch this hurdle is to use, abuse and exploit the themes and topics they are most interested in, which largely fall under the umbrella term of popular culture. Any time you can use images, examples, statistics or characters from the TV programmes, films or games they watch and play can only be a positive step forward.

A contentious yet significant issue we are all confronted with is the disparity between the results of boys and girls in schools and we must, as a response, try to differentiate our lessons in order to bridge this gap. Making use of popular culture that the boys in your class in question are familiar with and, even better, will respond to, is an excellent differentiation tool. When differentiating you are not only altering tasks and topics according to ability level; you are also differentiating to suit their interests. Get their attention and half the battle is won!

Use Bloom's Taxonomy

Benjamin Bloom's categorization of the levels of abstraction in questioning can be an excellent way to structure your class's enquiry into a given topic. Making explicit use of Bloom's Taxonomy is a very candid way of differentiating by outcome. Organize your activity to have students working through a series of mini-tasks that advance their progress through the taxonomy to higher-order thinking; let the class know which level you expect everyone to reach to ensure they all achieve a given standard and allow the students to work through this at their own pace. There is an element of challenge available to all, without just pointing a finger at your gifted and talented students and dumping extra work on them or pointing a finger at your SEN students and reducing their workload. Use Table 7.1 to help shape your tasks and questioning.

Table 7.1

Competence	Question tags	Sample activities
Knowledge	list, define, tell, describe, identify, show, label, collect, examine, quote, name, who, when, where	Make a timeline List the main events Make notes on ... Write an acrostic poem Label the parts of ... Find definitions for ... Find examples of ...
Comprehension	translate, contrast, summarize, describe, interpret, associate, distinguish, predict, estimate, differentiate, discuss	How is ... different from ... Explain ... in your own words Predict what will happen next Create a collage of images related to ... Create a flow chart Create a cartoon strip of ...
Application	solve, illustrate, classify, examine, construct, use, show, complete, modify	Create a model/diorama of ... Provide solutions for case studies 'Sell This Product!' (See Chapter 13) Use quotes from the story to show ...
Analysis	explain, analyse, separate, connect, arrange, divide, compare, select, infer, classify, order, investigate, contrast, categorize, distinguish	Design a questionnaire to show ... Create a diagram to show the important features of ... Write a review on ... Arrange these key terms into categories and explain their placement Break down ... into five easy-to-follow steps

| Synthesis | combine, modify, rearrange, substitute, plan, design, invent, what if?, compose, formulate, generalize, rewrite, integrate, create, prepare | Compose a poem in the style of ... Design a ... to improve ... Rewrite ... for a modern audience 'Plenary Pals' (see Chapter 4) Develop an advertising slogan for ... |
| Evaluation | prioritize, debate, judge, recommend, assess, discuss, rate, determine, select, argue, choose, justify, verify, decide | Rank the most important qualities of ... Prepare a list of criteria to judge a ... Plan a debate on ... Choose a celebrity who would be most suited to ... and explain why Write a letter of application for ... |

Use a variety of learning styles

Yes, we have all had at least one training day some time in the last five years that discussed the importance of preferred learning styles. What all these INSET days have shown us is that there are more theories behind it than you can shake your gold-plated cane at, and the bottom line is that different people learn in different ways. Before you roll your eyes and tear this page out of the book, there are a few things we can conclude when it comes to the whole learning styles gauntlet and some things we remind the students of as we poll their 'preferred learning style' for the seventh time in PSHE or 'Thinking Skills' or 'Learning to Learn' or 'Study Skills' or whatever your school happens to call it at the moment:

- Just because it is your 'preferred learning style' does not mean it is your ONLY learning style.

- Using a variety of learning styles is the best way for most people to learn.
- It is not possible to address every task or topic in every lesson with every learning style there is available.

A popular model, and perhaps the simplest, is VAK (visual, auditory, kinesthetic). Because lessons are not set (in any schools we have encountered, anyway) according to learning style, the best way to hedge your bets is to have a taste of everything in your lesson. Give them an opportunity to get out of their seats, even if it is only to move into groups or write an answer on the board. Use pictures or video clips if you can; we all love the hushed silence that falls over the room when the demi-god known as the TV is fired up. Oral quizzes and the articulating of ideas is something that happens in every lesson, isn't it? Obviously, you will not be able to provide for each style in perfect proportion, but you can at least show some provision throughout the course of the lesson. Be sure to identify in your lesson plan how you have considered and catered for a variety of learners in your class.

Use the 'short but sweet' principle

Very closely linked to the idea of catering to a variety of learning styles in the classroom, is structuring your lesson so that you have a series of short tasks. This ensures that you don't spend too long on any one task to avoid your class switching off and getting bored. It also provides more scope for squeezing in a range of learning styles. This is a vital principle to follow, especially if you have a class with limited attention spans.

Use picture books

OK, so some of you probably went into secondary teaching because you couldn't be doing with the cutesy, colour-coded wonders of the primary sector – but let us assure you, there are some little gems to be stolen from our primary colleagues, picture books being one of them. There are many picture books to be had out there that can be integrated into a secondary curriculum in very creative, interesting and fun ways. They have countless merits: they provide an accessible text for students with weak literacy skills, they are an excellent application of visual and oral learning styles and they address as wide a spectrum of issues and topics as any other source. The books do need to be carefully chosen, because a sure-fire way to have a tough class switch off is to make them feel you are patronizing them.

Picture books need not be saved for reluctant readers; your top set classes can be drawn in and will respond in sensitive and interesting ways to these little treasures as well. Though there are obvious links for many of the books that follow to history and English lessons, some really creative lessons could be developed for use in PSHE, art and drama. Hunt around and you will be pleasantly surprised at the picture books you can find to fit in with your discipline. The following is an annotated bibliography of a few of our favourites:

Yee, Paul. (1996), *Ghost Train*. Toronto: Groundwood Books.
This is the story of a Chinese peasant girl who is visited by the ghost of her father, a Chinese labourer in the mid-19th century who died building the railway in Canada. Her father implores her to paint the 'fire car' that rides the rails he helped build; her painting helps to transport home those who lost their lives during the construction of the railway.

Taylor, Clark (1992), *The House that Crack Built*. San Francisco: Chronicle Books.
Using the format of the well-known nursery rhyme 'The House that Jack Built', this story runs through the production, distribution and collateral damage of the crack industry.

Innocenti, Roberto and McEwan, Ian (1985), *Rose Blanche*. London: Random House.
This is a story about the Holocaust, told from the point of view of a young German girl. It has absolutely stunning pictures and a very poignant message.

Burleigh, Robert (1997), *Hoops*. New York: Silver Whistle Books.
A sensory experience and description of playing basketball.
Brilliant illustration and is sure to capture the attention of the
sporty boys in your class.

Tsuchiya,Y. *et al.* (1988), *Faithful Elephant: A True Story of Animals,
People and War*. Boston: Houghton Mifflin Company.
A true story of three elephants that were put to death because of
World War II, this story looks at the pain and anguish brought
about through war.

Granfield, L. (2000), *In Flanders Fields: The Story of the Poem by
John McCrae*. Toronto: Fitzhenry & Whiteside.
Based on the famous World War I poem 'In Flanders Fields', this
is a beautifully illustrated book that would complement the study
of World War I or any wartime literature.

Bunting, E. (1996), *Someday a Tree*. Boston: Clarion Books.
This book deals with the effects of pollution on the environment
and one girl's attempt to fight it.

Use your support assistants

If you are one of the lucky ones that has a support or teaching
assistant in your classroom, it is important that you make the
most of them, as this is a key area of scrutiny for your
observer. Here are some tips about making the most of your
support assistants and the differentiation opportunities they
provide:

- Talk to them often in the lesson. Ask them for their opinions
  and have them visibly assist you with the organization of the
  lesson for such things as assigning groups, choosing people to
  respond to questions or to share their work with the class. Not
  only will your TA feel useful and included in the lesson, you
  will also raise their profile with the students in your
  classroom.

- Use your support assistants to trick the children. Though this sounds devious and horrible, it is not. If you can afford a little rehearsal time with your TA, you can pull some fantastic heists that really hit a point home and grab your class' attention! Upon arriving at a new school, there were rumours floating around that one of the members of the English Department was able to read minds. In truth, the teacher and the TA had conferred before the lesson and when the teacher asked for a volunteer to choose a number between one and one thousand the TA was only too happy to comply. For authenticity, the TA had to tell their secret number (which had been pre-agreed) to the child beside them. After much hocus-pocus and the correct number guessed, the teacher had developed loads of street cred with her class and was able to generate a fantastic buzz for the ensuing lesson on Harry Potter.

- Just because a support assistant is there for a designated child does not mean that they must be glued to their side, or even sat next to them. Some students prefer not to sit next to their TA and will ask for help when they want it. You can ensure that your TA is sat in proximity to the students you know need help, or you can ask them to circulate and oversee a specific list of children. It is a positive thing to not have them stuck in one place all the time, as the students around them can become too dependent and unwilling to work in their absence.

Use interesting extension tasks

We'll say it because we know you are all thinking it: it is annoying when you have planned a lesson that is 100 per cent suitable for 95 per cent of your class and that lone ranger from the back row proudly stomps up to you while you are trying to explain the task to 'Jake' for the seventh time and proclaims 'I'm done!'. Of course you are pleased that this student has engaged with the task so quickly and efficiently, but there is that little voice inside you that calls: 'For the love of all things evil and unwholesome, what will I do with them now?' If you have read ahead to the 'Trash it!' section in this chapter, you will already know how we feel about extra worksheets: they stink. The first obvious extension task to set them is to have a quick look through their work and send them back to fix mistakes, fill in bits they missed or expand sections that could use development. After that, the work you set them should be stimulating and interesting, yet self-directed as you still have 28 other smiling faces that need assistance through the initial task. Here, hopefully, are a few ideas to engage your star pupil and leave you to tend to the rest of your flock:

- Lateral thinking puzzles are always a good thing to keep on hand; students generally like to give them a try and LOVE to tell their friends when they crack it. You can often adapt them to make them fit your topic.
- See 'Plenary Pals' in Chapter 4; this is a great way to keep your eagles busy!
- Display work (either designing or helping you to put up a new display) can be a great way to keep them busy, challenged, and pleased about the task you have given them.
- If you have a computer available in your classroom, setting some relevant research work or directing them to a pertinent website is a great reward and a means of stretching their learning.
- Have a list of 'challenge tasks' so that they can choose from some of the higher-order levels of Bloom's Taxonomy. Even if they are not specifically topical to what you are studying at the moment, it is a worthwhile extension activity if it practises and stretches skills that are necessary to your discipline. The element of choice removes it from the 'extra worksheet' cardinal sin.

Trash it!

Not all differentiation techniques are created equal and the following rotten tomatoes fall way short of the supermarket:

- **Colour-coded differentiated worksheets.** It takes the class no time at all to figure out that the clever kids have the blue sheets and the less-than-clever kids have the orange ones. Would you ever stand at the front of the room and shout 'Can you put your hand up if you aren't very clever?'. No. So just don't do it with the worksheets.
- **Heaping extra work on those that finish early.** Punishing your high-flyers with heaps of boring work whenever they get done early is no way to encourage them or to stretch their potential. They will quickly suss what is going on and a) start working at a slower pace; or b) quietly sit there and do nothing to avoid their third worksheet on using semicolons.
- **Having them 'colour around the outside' when they are done.** A story from one of our colleagues' childhood experiences is called to mind. Her primary school class had been given a picture of a cow to decorate and colour in. While all the other happy five year olds were making them rainbow-shaded, or covered in hearts and flowers, this particular student had made several sensible brown blobs, coloured them in uniformly, and called it done. When she approached the teacher for something else to do, the teacher insisted she colour in the rest of the cow, despite protests about that not being the kind of cow she wanted to create. Moral of the story: your students will end up dissatisfied with mindless busy work and will still be talking about it twenty-five years later.

Though it's been mentioned several times, one of the biggest things to remember when considering differentiation is to make sure that you include explicit mention of all the fabulous techniques you use; if you are not going to toot your own horn, no one else will either. So toot away, and consult Chapter 3 for some big and clever ideas about how to get it done.

8

Pimp Your . . . Literacy Focus

> You teach a child to read, and he or her will be able to pass a literacy test.
>
> George W. Bush, on education reform,
> 21 February 2001

One sure way to convince your examiner that you are not only an excellent teacher but also out to save the youth of today, modern society and the planet in general, is to show that you have thought about how to help develop pupils' literacy skills within the lesson in question. This has to mean more than simply writing on your lesson plan 'Literacy: lesson includes both reading and writing'. Literacy is an integral part of any teaching because, as people often forget, as well as reading and writing, literacy refers to the use of spoken language too.

Sometimes it is difficult to articulate exactly how you are providing opportunities to develop literacy skills, so we have compiled a ready-to-go list of cross-curricular examples for you. Chances are, one of the jewels below will nestle snugly into your lesson plan.

Literacy element gems to take away

Reading

- After reading the text, pupils will be invited to underline any words that they do not fully understand. These words will then be discussed as a class.
- The longer text will be presented to pupils in a series of small sections to prevent pupils from feeling over-faced and to allow them to assimilate the information more effectively.
- Using highlighters, pupils will be asked to identify what they feel to be the most important points in the text. This will require them to practise scanning a text for relevant information.
- Rather than copying information, the teacher will show pupils how to summarize it by modelling the process on the classroom board.

- Pupils will be allocated time to read through a partner's piece of work, identify successes and make suggestions for how the piece might be improved.
- Pupils will be required to sequence a disjointed text during the starter activity.
- Pupils are routinely allowed 5 minutes at the beginning of the lesson to proofread their own written homework and make any necessary corrections before they submit it to the teacher.

Writing

- Pupils will be issued with a good/bad example of the writing they are being asked to produce. Pupils will then be encouraged to identify, by implication, what they will need to do in order to produce a high-quality piece of work.
- Using suggestions from pupils, the teacher will build up a short example of the type of writing that is required, thereby breaking down and modelling the process for their pupils.
- Pupils will be given precise instructions about the purpose and the audience of their work. Pupils will then be required to adapt style, structure and vocabulary appropriately.
- A writing frame (an example of which can be found at the end of this chapter) will be provided to help pupils to structure their work and to make the extended writing task seem less overwhelming.
- Pupils will be encouraged to develop their own writing frame (an example of which can be found at the end of this chapter) in preparation for completing the written task. Pupils will be asked to consider their past experience of writing frames in order to create their own.
- As well as paying close attention to the content of their work, pupils will be encouraged to redraft their work to correct mistakes in spelling, grammar and punctuation.
- A particular literacy focus, for example writing in paragraphs, writing in sentences, checking spelling with a dictionary, etc., is announced at the beginning of the lesson alongside the primary learning objective.

Speaking and listening

- During the plenary, pupils will be assisted to articulate verbally what they have learned.
- As paired group-work commences, pupils will be encouraged to discuss and negotiate what they will need to do in order to succeed in the task.
- All pupils will be encouraged and expected to contribute to a structured class discussion. This will enable them to practise articulating their ideas clearly and with confidence, responding to and building on the ideas of others.
- To facilitate the clear, purposeful feedback of ideas, pupils will be issued with a speaking frame (an example of which can be found at the end of this chapter, Figure 8.1) to help them to organize their ideas in a way which will be effective for a listening audience.

Keywords

- Key subject-specific vocabulary will be introduced clearly at the beginning of the lesson, used during the lesson and revisited at the end.
- There will be a clear focus on the imperative verbs that pupils will encounter in their exam, for example *compare, calculate, describe, predict, explain, argue, analyse, etc.*
- Pupils will be encouraged to use key connectives to assist the flow of their work, for example *moreover, however, similarly, especially, although, etc.*
- Using pupils' suggestions, the teacher will build up a bank of relevant keywords on the board that pupils can make use of in their own work.
- The teacher will hold up relevant keywords on cards at times when acoustics are problematic, such as outdoors.
- Mnemonics (an example of which can be found at the end of this chapter, Figure 8.2) will be used to help pupils to remember difficult spellings. Pupils may be asked to invent their own mnemonic.

Trash it!

The two Rs

Our principal advice to you on things to avoid when promoting the literacy element of your lesson is against making the common mistake of trying to pass off *any* reading or writing activity in the lesson as evidence of your helping pupils to develop their literacy skills. Requiring pupils to read or write something should never be confused with actually actively helping to enhance and improve their literacy skills. The latter needs far more complex thought and planning.

Spelling/Grammar/Punctuation mistakes on the board or learning resource

Teacher applicants have failed to be called for interview because they spelled 'sincerely' wrong in their letter of application; long-standing teachers have been chewed out by parents because they missed an apostrophe out of a child's report. How, therefore, can you expect to receive an 'Outstanding' rating for a lesson when there is a big, bloomin' blooper sticking out of it? What's more, if an officious observer can't find anything else wrong with your lesson, they may quite possibly take great delight in pointing out your punctuation mistake.

It's all about appearances: a spelling, punctuation or grammar mistake on your resource, board or lesson plan spoils the flawless face of your lesson. It's like turning up for a hot date with a great bulging zit on your face that you haven't bothered to squeeze; or worse: turning up to your gran's house without a scarf to cover that lovebite. It's tacky, it gives the wrong impression and, frankly, you're worth more than that.

Oh, and one last thing

Put the cloze procedures down and step away from the wordsearches – it's for your own good.

Writing about a school trip

When we first arrived, we noticed that . . .

Next we visited the . . . . and discovered that . . .

For lunch, we decided to . . .

In the afternoon, I was interested to learn that . . .

My favourite part of the trip was . . . . because . . .

Sentence stems to aid discussion

- Have you ever considered . . .?
- I find it really interesting that . . .
- What makes you think that . . .?
- I feel very strongly that . . .
- Do you agree that . . .?
- Something that I find difficult to understand is . . .
- This makes me think of . . .
- How do you feel about . . .?
- It could be argued that . . .. However, I believe . . .
- It is certainly true to say that . . .
- Before we can answer this question, I think we need to . . .

Figure 8.1

Writing to argue or persuade

When you have to write to ARGUE or PERSUADE, it is useful to follow the FEET mnemonic to help you structure your work, for example:

Should smoking be banned in public places?

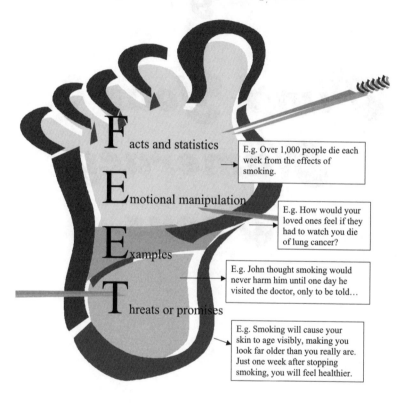

Figure 8.2

9

Pimp Your . . .
Numeracy
Focus

If I didn't have some kind of education, then I wouldn't be able to count my money.

Missy Elliott

Showing your observer that you feel teachers of all subjects are responsible for promoting and extending pupils' numeracy skills is guaranteed to go down well. Numeracy is another essential communication skill alongside literacy, and has been a statutory element of secondary school cross-curricular provision since September 2001. Having said that, unless you work for a school that has mathematics and computing specialist status, it may be that your school does not require you to include a numeracy focus in your lesson plan. However, if it can comfortably form an additional learning opportunity in your lesson, then it is a sure-fire way to further humble your observer under the glowing light of your general prowess in the classroom.

In their published advice regarding numeracy across the curriculum, the DfES (www.dfes.gov.uk) tells us that the 'three priorities' are:

1. to improve accuracy, especially in calculation, measurement and graphical work;
2. to improve interpretation and presentation of graphs, charts and diagrams;
3. to improve reasoning and problem solving.

Teachers of some subjects will certainly struggle more than others with this, so the following suggestions are especially for those of you who have been asked to attend to the development of numeracy skills in your lesson and are at a total loss for what to do. Yes, you – the one sitting there with the hard-done-by expression on your face because the last time a calculator was used in your classroom, you were checking how many hours of school were left before the summer holidays.

-   Draw pupils' attention to the number of marks allocated to particular questions in their upcoming exam/test and the amount of time that they are given to complete the entire exam. Then ask them to calculate the amount of time they should spend on each question, in the light of this information.

- Allow pupils to take a class opinion poll on a particular debate topic and ask them to convey this as a chart or graph.
- Ask pupils to produce a storyboard for a particular sequence of events, thus requiring them to divide their page equally into eight carefully measured boxes.
- When studying poetry, encourage pupils to examine the *rhythm* in the poem, in particular identifying any discrepancies in the number of beats or syllables.
- When dividing the class into equal groups, ask the class to count the number of pupils present and work out the sum for you.
- During quizzes and competitions, encourage pupils to keep score. Use a variety of formats for gaining marks; for example, in the style of well-known TV quizzes such as *Who Wants to Be a Millionaire?*, where money is doubled at certain points, or *The Weakest Link*, where the counter returns to zero each time the points are 'banked'.

Trash it!

Stuffing it in

As you can see, it is possible simply to emphasize certain aspects of your lesson that you previously hadn't necessarily labelled as 'numerical' in your own head. However, we would definitely advise against forcibly inserting an uncomfortably large numeracy element into your poor maxed-out lesson plan unless your observer really has a particular penchant for the whole numeracy thing.

Lame attempts

Don't even think about passing off any of the following as a significant contribution to raising standards in numeracy skills among the youth of today:

- 'Draw a margin around your work.'
- 'Write between 100 and 150 words.'
- 'If you've finished, go sit back down and count the number of words you have written.'
- 'Write the date in your book.'

10

Pimp Your . . . Information and Communication Technology

> The secret of teaching is to appear to have known all your
> life what you just learned this morning.
>
> Ron Edelen

Before we even get started here, there will need to be a little disclaimer. If you are one of the privileged individuals who:

- has a computer suite in or adjacent to your classroom, at your disposal;
- has the GIFT of an interactive whiteboard or data projector;
- has a lesson planned which involves using a computer suite;

this chapter might not be for you. Instead, we will be catering to the underclass: those of us who still have to write on a whiteboard (or, heaven forbid, a blackboard), or have to schedule our use of computers in advance and rely on the good-old overhead projector for images we want to share with our class. Yes, we are the ones in need of fancy ways to show off our Information and Communication Technology (ICT) prowess. If you have any of the above points at your disposal and cannot think of ways to incorporate ICT in your lesson, then you will need much more than a chapter in a book to help you out of that little situation.

For those of us outside these categories, we mustn't go ostrich and pretend that ICT is not a part of our teaching responsibility because we are without these advantages and because we are not teaching an ICT lesson ('It's geography, dammit!'). This echoes the cries of English teachers who insist you CANNOT incorporate numeracy in an English lesson and PE teachers who insist literacy is IMPOSSIBLE to include in their discipline. Awkward at times? Yes. Feels somewhat forced? Yes. Makes you want to drive spikes under your fingernails and sing the hokey-cokey at the top of your lungs? Hopefully not. Though it may not be as explicit as having the whole class visit a website of topical relevance, or using a PowerPoint presentation, there are indeed relevant and useful ways to squirm a seed of ICT into your Dark-Ages classroom.

A couple of pointers before we get into the ideas:

- Check out your school's ICT policy and perhaps the schemes of work each year group is following. This should be available from your ICT coordinator. This will give you an idea of what skills and knowledge your students already have, or will be developing at the moment. Showing evidence of this kind of knowledge is one of the key things Ofsted look for when inspecting ICT.
- Look into what ICT provisions are available for students who do not have computers or the internet at home. This can make homework or outside-class research tricky.
- Make sure you are COMPLETELY familiar with the technology and equipment that you are using. In an average, everyday lesson it is OK to play on the expertise and technological prowess of your students, but in an observation situation you need to look comfortable and confident with the technology you have chosen. Be prepared not only to use the equipment, but also to troubleshoot if your students run into problems.

Homework

Ahh, sweet homework! Both the albatross and the ace of the teaching world. You want to scream when you set something that only 45 per cent of the class complete, but want to dance and sing when your little treasures go that extra mile and surprise you with homework that they actually didn't do on the bus and/or spent longer than four minutes on. Homework can be the ideal way to make sure that you are using ICT in your lesson.

To really show your proficiency, your ICT homework should be very explicitly and carefully planned; avoid at all costs 'For homework I want you to research ... on the internet'. This can be a frustrating experience for the student, as there are surely umpteen-million websites on any given topic you may be looking at. This sort of unfocused task will most likely result in the student printing off five pages of information that they have cut and pasted, but probably not read. Focus your task to a list of no more than three websites that they should consult, and be sure that you know ahead of time what information they should be gleaning. Send the students home with a short description of the task typed up, complete with the relevant website addresses. This way there will be no cries of 'I didn't know what to do' when it comes time for collection. Whether you use the researched information in the observation lesson, or you opt to set the homework that lesson, either way will be an explicit and well-planned use of ICT for your observer to see. As mentioned above, be sure to look into options for students who do not have access to the internet or computers at home.

Digital cameras

Digital cameras count as ICT! Most schools will have a supply of them in one department or another, even if they are not made available to the masses. Heck, bring in your own if the school doesn't have one you can use! There are many fantastically creative things you can do with a digital camera in your lesson. For example:

- Have students take pictures of developmental stages of a project.
- Have a student take pictures during the lesson to use for display purposes later.
- Use images taken in a previous lesson for students to analyse performance.
- Have students annotate pictures taken of themselves or their work/project in a previous lesson.
- Use images printed onto OHP transparencies as a part of your plenary session (provided you have printing facilities) to recapture important points in the lesson.

The opportunities are endless and at least the equipment is easy to use, transport and obtain.

Web page design

No, we've not forgotten that this chapter is dedicated to those struggling with the ABSENCE of a computer. Using a twist on the old 'design a poster that shows . . .', you can have your class design a home page (with a pencil and paper, obviously) for a website that would provide information about the topic you are studying. This can be a great way to consolidate ideas and sub-topics that are pertinent. By having them include tabs for different areas of the page, text boxes, important headings and even the all-important website address, you are making use of conventions of this vital medium in the absence of the computers themselves. Be sure to have an OHP or photocopy of a well-designed home page for students to use for reference and inspiration.

One-computer wonder . . .

Most of us have at least one machine, or could blag ourselves at least one, possibly two, laptop(s) if we needed to. Even this limited number of machines could be very useful in wedging that ICT kernel into your lesson. During group-work tasks, you could plan a highly structured, 5-minute task on the computer or internet that pupils perform in small groups. Whether this is a quick 'fact hunt' on a given website, a search for key terms, or a mad hunt to find two good websites that could be consulted for future reference, you are providing a worthwhile, albeit brief, ICT opportunity for your class. Such a quick blast and limited time on the computer also nixes any messing about or wasting time on irrelevant sites!

One day laptops will replace grungy exercise books, white-boards will be found only in museums and we will have robots that take the lessons as we control them from a remote location. Until that day is realized, we must do what we can with what we've got and muddle through our ICT inclusion as best we can. It's no great secret that we don't all have fabulous ICT resources at our disposal all the time (a further POX on you that do!), but it is a feather in your hat if you can show awareness, under-standing and willingness to work with what's available. Or, if all else fails, you can do the ostrich thing . . .

That's two independent thought alarms in one day. Willie, the children are over-stimulated. Remove all the colored chalk from the classrooms.

Principal Seymour Skinner, *The Simpsons*

You walk up to your pigeon-hole on Monday morning with a cheerless gait as you lament the jobs you did not get done over the weekend. Year 7 exercise books are still not marked, you didn't paint your garage door and still have not 'scooped the poops' your sister's dog left in your garden two weeks ago. Hoping to find nothing more than a planner you have to return to 'Jake' in your form (that kid would lose his head if it wasn't screwed on and he didn't need it for underage drinking) and perhaps this week's bulletin, you are faced with THREE forms to complete. The first one is asking you to review the course you went on last week; the second requests your views and opinions on the up-and-coming end-of-term assembly (at which your offer to sing 'Another Brick in The Wall' is respectfully declined); and the third is from the Assessment for Learning focus group, kindly asking for your applications of AfL by 10:30 this morning. Do you feel angry just reading this? Well, imagine how your students feel as you plop down a barrage of worksheets of a similar interest level to the ones you just dug out of your pigeon-hole and ask them to work through them with enthusiasm and care for the next half an hour. Hence the importance of this chapter ... making those resources more exciting than the pigeon-hole drivel we all lament.

You do not HAVE to create your own resources. A good portion of your departmental budget is undoubtedly spent each year on purchasing items that will save you from having to develop all of your own. It's all part of the whole 'don't re-invent the wheel' concept. We all have our favourite resources that we use and use again; it's like a comfort blanket (the rest of you still have comfort blankets too, right?) that gets the job done well every time and feels good while you do it. We, however, are not talking about the lessons that you are fortunate enough to be able to deliver time and time again or the resources that accompany them ... we are looking at ways to pimp your lesson, and resources is a fantastic place to start.

There are times when you happen upon a brilliant resource, or, when genius strikes, you design the perfect resource that shapes an entire ensuing lesson. There are the other times when you have a fantastic idea about how you want to teach something and how a lesson should play out and the resource is nowhere to be found. It is times like these that you have to place your comfort blanket, we mean trusty folders and pre-fab resources, to one side and prepare to pimp your OWN materials. The advantages to preparing your own are endless: they are laid out and presented in the exact way YOU want them to be; the ideas are phrased in a manner that will suit the group you have designed them for; they are set out by you to teach the given topic in the way that *you* see best, not by some hopped-up, control-freak teacher who *thinks* they are so wonderful that they deserve to be published (uh ... scratch that last comment) ... you see where we are going.

Sometimes it can feel as if the resources you use in the lesson are like the goody bag at the end of a children's party. You know you've got it right when the observer requests permission to take your creations away with them, and you probably feel unreasonably indignant when the observer chooses instead to disdainfully leave them lying on a desk at the back of your room when they walk out. Resources can be a sensitive subject for teachers. We are all kind, generous souls, but sometimes casting our little brainchildren out into the hands of others can make us feel territorial and possessive. Call it parental instinct. We expect that, like us, you have had that experience of handing over to a colleague your painstaking creations, your paper-babies, only to receive in return a stack of free printable resources from teachcrap.com. And then your blood starts to boil, doesn't it? Those idea-stealing colleagues who offer nothing in return become masked, gloved menaces, sneaking through your filing cabinets in the dead of night. No? OK, so it's just us who have issues, but we bet you've taken to drawing a big 'C' inside a circle at the bottom of your worksheet at least once in your career ...

Take heart: it's the difference your resources make to the kids that really matters, isn't it? And if that's not solace enough, at least when you are inspected, the time and effort that you put into designing and producing your own resources will actually pay off. Plus, if your resources are pimperrific you don't feel so bad when you accidentally run off 100 more copies than you meant to on that damn touch-sensitive photocopier.

When it came to teaching-resources, there was no better designer than Cool Dogg Jr. He was the Ralph Lauren of the Teaching World. Every worksheet or stimulus was breathtakingly well presented and ever-successful in achieving its aim. At first Cool Dogg Jr was flattered by the admiration he obviously attracted from the vacuous teacher down the corridor. He was pleased to settle her classes down for her when they were 'doing her head in' or fix the bottom drawer on her filing cabinet to save her breaking a nail. He even shared some of his pimped-to-perfection home-made resources with her. It wasn't until he caught her at a department meeting trying to pass off one of his entire schemes of work as her own, that Cool Dogg Jr began to feel a little indignant. From then on, Cool decided to keep the 'Eight Great Tips for Producing Pimped-up Resources' entirely secret, to be shared only with fellow pimpers such as yourselves.

Here they are. Check carefully to see who is looking over your shoulder, and after reading these pages, be sure to eat them.

Eight Great Tips for Producing Pimped-up Resources

1. Always include the learning objective on your resource

This is a useful little pimping technique, which shows that you are just that bit sharper than those people whose resources look fab, but you're never quite sure how or when to use them. It's also an in-your-face way to reiterate the learning objective for the pupils especially if, in your nervousness, you forget to write it up on the board. You are less likely to have to explain another 30 times what you want the pupils to do when the purpose of the exercise is right there in front of their noses.

2. *Always word-process your resource*

We know this is an obvious one, but we also know that there are some pimptastic teachers out there who still just love the look of their own handwriting. We are sure it is attractive too, but there is just something about a handwritten resource that suggests, a) you just knocked it up five minutes before the end of breaktime; or b) it's one you've kept from your own schooldays because you're hoping the vibes from your first favourite teacher will bring you good luck.

Type it up in a clear, easy-to-read font and it will be immortalized.

3. *Always personalize the resource for this specific group of pupils*

This is where the whole 'got it saved on my hard-drive' triumph really comes into play. Each time you use the resource, you can make it personally relevant for the pupils. For example, include the pupils' names, cartoon impressions of them, insider jokes which only your class will 'get' and which will make them feel quite special. You might even like to feature a different member of the class on each resource that you make. This way, by the time your observation lesson comes round, the pupils are scrambling to get their hands on those resources to see which of their classmates' endearing idiosyncrasies are being celebrated today.

4. *Always make your resources attractive as well as functional*

If your granny knits you a big Mark Darcy jumper that is sure to keep you nice and warm, you'll probably still be reluctant to make use of it when the winter months come. Pupils are no less discerning when it comes to learning resources. They will consciously or unconsciously make a snap decision about the work they are faced with based on what it looks like. This is where your devious designing comes in. You are (hopefully) smarter than they are, so get to work manipulating their minds with your presentational devices. Want to make long division appear more interesting? Do one of the following ...

a) Include relevant images on the sheet, a caricature of yourself, for example, complete with a speech bubble containing your best-known catchphrase. Indeed, speech or thought bubbles are useful for making any celebrity appear relevant to your worksheet. Try and picture, for example, David Beckham attempting to divide the number of players in his team with the number of half-time orange segments ...

b) Ensure that nothing on the resource looks daunting. We've all heard pupils exclaim in dismay, 'Have I got to read all that?!' or seen them fight over the only book on the library shelf that contains pictures. Break up any long pieces of text into easily digestible chunks. Make use of borders, boxes and different fonts, and never use single spacing or a font smaller than 14pt – you might fail to tick the differentiation box because you haven't catered for less confident readers ...

c) If you are not already a convert, consider using a laminator to preserve your best resources and make the pupils (and your observer!) feel really spoilt. However, if you are a laminator virgin, we should warn you that this practice can be highly addictive. Even if you haven't already been caught in school well after work hours laminating unnecessary things, you can usually spot the ones who have because their timetables are laminated and stuck to the front of their teaching files. Many a great teacher has fallen victim to the growing 'laminate to glaminate' obsession. Know when to stop. You can have too much of a good thing ...

d) Photocopy your resource onto brightly coloured paper. (Well, it might impress some of the pupils and your observer, for a while, at least ...)

5. *Always include examples that the pupils can refer to*

Just when you thought it was safe to leave the pupils to their independent work and begin circulating among them – reducing the observer to tears with your sensitive guidance and inspiring suggestions – ten hands shoot up in the air and an echo of 'I don't get what we are supposed to be doing' reverberates around the classroom. Sometimes it doesn't matter how many times you explain it; the pupils need a visual reminder right there in front of them all the time, slap bang in the middle of the page. This is why, for an observation lesson, we would strongly advise you to include a ready-completed example on the sheet. This could simply mean filling in the first answer for them in the manner you would like it to be set out, or you might prefer to provide an example of an A-grade/C-grade/level 5, etc. response to the first question. A clear example is often all that is needed to ensure that a pupil finally grasps a concept.

It is also worth mentioning here that any worksheet should still require pupils to engage with the rest of the lesson in order to succeed in completing the task. Handing out a worksheet that requires pupils to 'simply get on with it' (such as we have all encountered when covering for ill colleagues) would be a sure-fire way to drop clumsily to a 'Satisfactory' in the resource department. An outstanding resource inspires and facilitates learning; it does not just provide a frame in which prior learning can be showcased.

6. *Always remember, there's more to resources than worksheets*

A pimping expert is always on the lookout for things to use in the classroom. It might be a thought-provoking picture or object, or a short film clip or TV advert, a model, a photograph; the possibilities are endless. Visual aids can work wonders for capturing your class's attention at the beginning of the lesson, and what's more, pupils love to learn more about you and your life. Bringing in something relevant from your own life to show your class often really inspires interest and will impress your observer. For example, if you wanted to illustrate how advertising impacts on our lives, you might bring in a collection of items you had been foolish enough to buy after seeing them advertised on TV. A pimped history teacher we know who was teaching her pupils about life during World War I, took the time to look up wartime recipes and cooked up a few strange dishes for the pupils to taste and comment on. Of course, the delighted Ofsted inspector graded her lesson as 'Outstanding', possibly partly for the sheer dedication and originality it demonstrated.

7. Always make use of current media coverage of a subject

If you look hard enough, you will be able to find a current story in the media which relates to your topic. If you are teaching pupils about a particular religion, throw those textbooks in a cupboard and find a story involving people of the same faith in the news. If pupils are studying a medical condition such as anorexia, find a celebrity's account of their own battle with the disorder.

8. Always use real, live texts where possible

It is all too easy to rely on the ready-provided documents we find in textbooks: a pretend description of a fictional holiday resort, the imaginary mathematical problem of an imaginary person, a made-up speech from a made-up politician. Yet it is possible to provide your pupils with real, live examples of all of these texts. Knowing that they are studying something authentic and current, something which they have probably already heard a little about, is a big motivator for pupils.

So consider, just for a lesson or two, putting aside the epic poetry and bringing in some song lyrics. Think about doing away with the textbook diagrams of football matches, and looking at how the England Boys do it. It's different, it's exciting, and it'll get you a lot nearer to the 'Outstanding' mark than that 'Learning Made Easy but Strangely Tedious' textbook, Volume 3.

So there you have it – eight easy ways to ensure your resources are pimped to perfection. Sorry for revealing your secret, Cool Dogg; but we doubt your Little Miss Resource Stealer would be able to tear herself away from her 'How to Be Adequate' survival guide in order to read this book anyway.

Trash it!

Resources someone else designed for a completely different class

Although there are some superb teaching and learning resources freely available on the internet – and let us be the first to say we've found them, used them, and inwardly sung our gratitude to the generous souls who took the time to share them – there really is nothing as impressive as a completely original, made-to-measure resource produced by the teacher themselves. Let's face it: the odds against somebody else's resource being perfect for your own class are really quite high. Instead, demonstrate your dedication and innovation by issuing your pupils with a resource that has pimp written all over it. (No, not literally. We're talking about the need to PREPARE, INNOVATE, MOTIVATE and PERFECT!)

Antique worksheets

If you are using an old, reliable worksheet, be sure to check the date at the bottom of it. An ancient resource (no matter how 'hip' you still think it is) will not convince the observer that you are great at moving with the times and embracing new teaching styles and concepts. Similarly, for a pupil, 'made in 1998' may as well say 'made in the olden days when everything and everyone was a little more boring'. Find your Tippex and head for the Reprographics Department.

12

Pimp Your ...
Starter
Activity

For every person who wants to teach there are approximately thirty people who don't want to learn – much.
W.C. Sellar and R.J. Yeatman, *And Now All This*

First impressions really do count. Imagine yourself at a party where no one speaks to you for the first ten minutes. Imagine a dinner party where the starter is Brussels sprouts. Imagine a first date that burps AND farts before you even leave the house. All of these are poor ways to begin potentially great events. Who cares how the rest of it goes once you've gotten off to a lousy start?

We regularly tell our pupils that their front pages/first paragraphs are the first thing an examiner sees and therefore they need to be impressive. With lesson starters, it's the same. If you've ever been an examiner, you'll know that more often than not you semi-consciously begin to gauge the essay's grade after reading the first two paragraphs. So take your own good advice and put the examiner in a good mood right from the beginning with a flamboyant and shiny starter.

Starter activities, despite what documents may suggest, were not invented in the 1990s. Before the National Strategy gently suggested (like a two by four around the head) that Key Stage 3 lessons should have three parts, effective practitioners knew that an exciting and interactive activity to begin the lesson will engage the interest and brighten the mood of the pupils. An inspiring starter is a great way to capture the heart and mind of your observer; a perfect opportunity to establish what a fun-loving, dynamic, risk-taking and generally impressive practitioner you are. It signals immediately to the observer that you don't work the same block as those teachers who shy away from activities involving whole-class interaction for fear it may result in a deterioration of pupil behaviour. Therefore steer well clear of mundane activities such as filling in blanks, worksheets or straightforward question and answer sessions.

To get some important boxes ticked, your lesson starter needs to do the following things:

- Deliver teaching objectives that have been nationally specified for this year group in this subject. (Try to relate them specifically to the National Framework or exam board assessment criteria, both in your lesson plan and when you introduce the activity to the pupils.)

- Inspire pupils to become actively involved in the lesson from the outset (or force them to if necessary!).
- Be pitched at an appropriate level to challenge all pupils.
- Maintain a sense of pace that encourages pupils to remain ontask and focused on what they are learning.

It is also worth pointing out that, although your lesson starter does not officially need to 'lead straight into the main part of the lesson that follows' (www.standards.dfes.gov.uk), if you are being observed for one lesson it would be advisable for there to be an obvious and clever link between the starter and the main thrust of the lesson, so that your pupils engage immediately with the core learning objectives in your lesson plan.

Other than being a turbo-powered, leather-seated vehicle for impressing the observer, a starter activity also serves a number of invaluable purposes, the most important of which being that it is an effective way to engage your pupils' interest and imagination and get them onside for the rest of the lesson. Pupils' concentration levels are often at their highest at the beginning of a lesson, following the stimulating physical activity of breaktime or of simply moving from one classroom to another. It is, therefore, a key moment to cash in on their heightened receptiveness to new information; you must entice them into a whole lesson's worth of learning. Don't waste this valuable window with mundane tasks such as taking a register or handing back homework. In fact, it is advisable, if time allows, to ensure that everything required for your lesson is already in place on desks before your observation lesson begins.

You can also use your starter activity as a means of differentiation – a way of catering for a particular learning style that would otherwise be somewhat sidelined during the lesson. You might even have a case for arguing that your super-stunning, interactive starter is specifically designed to help focus the minds of less motivated learners ...

Rothsteiny Vicious had barely settled into her first week as a newly qualified teacher when she learned that the headteacher intended to observe all new teachers before their first half-term holiday in October. Her colleagues were cynical when Rothsteiny questioned them about their leader and his tendencies as an observer. 'He's got I.O.D', her head of department told her, 'Initiative Obsession Disorder. Every time there's a new government initiative or, worse still, he goes on a COURSE, you can guarantee that he'll focus exclusively on that when he observes you. Forget how effective every other aspect of the lesson is ...'

Rothsteiny couldn't help feeling that maybe her HoD had been less than pleased with the outcome of his own assessment the last time he, himself, had been observed by the head. Nevertheless, Rothsteiny Vicious made good use of this information and was able to find out, via the staffroom gossip chain, that the headteacher was currently afflicted with an unhealthy obsession for starter activities.

To ensure that Rothsteiny would blow her observer away in the first ten minutes of the lesson, we gave her the following list of clever little tricks to choose from to get her lesson off to a stonking-good start.

The Beach Ball Trick

This has the clever effect of convincing pupils that they are having an excitingly inappropriate amount of fun in the classroom, while at the same time consolidating and extending their learning. The idea is that whoever catches the beach ball must make a relevant contribution to the activity. This activity can encourage even the most reluctant learners to contribute in a fun and non-threatening manner. The possibilities for use of this simple little strategy are endless. Here are just a few examples:

- To recap on German vocabulary learned last lesson: one pupil calls out a word in German and throws the ball. The classmate who catches the ball must translate the word into English and then call out another German word before passing on the ball again, and so on. This can also be used for counting up to 100 in a different language, each pupil calling out the next number in sequence as the ball is passed from person to person.
- To liven up the revision of multiplication tables: the beach ball is passed from one pupil to another, each pupil calling out the next number in the multiplication sequence as they catch the ball and pass it on.
- To summarize the plot of a novel or play: as each pupil catches the beach ball they announce the next important development in the sequence of events, before passing the ball on.

Uninvited Guests

You need some confident little show-offs for this one, but once they become familiar with the activity it can provide a hilarious and upbeat start to the learning, that may even gradually wipe out tardiness to your lessons.

One pupil waits outside the classroom while three volunteers are chosen to play uninvited guests at her party. Each of these guests is given an unusual character trait which dramatizes a key focus of the lesson. The first pupil then re-enters the room to play the host of a party. At a given cue from the teacher, each guest enters the party in turn and proceeds to display their unusual character trait in an increasingly shameless way. When the teacher signals for the action to cease, the host must guess the instructions their guests were acting under.

The beauty of this exercise lies in the dramatic irony. By allowing the rest of the class in on the secret traits of the guests, it ensures that their interest and amusement is maintained throughout the activity. What's more, it can be used for demonstrating specific skills or for exploring a particular theme or idea. Depending on the subject and lesson content, personality traits such as the following could be attributed:

- English: someone who can speak only in rhyme; a character or an aspect of a character from a novel
- science: someone who is magnetic to certain metals; an invertebrate; a particular insect
- history: a historical character or aspect of a historical character
- geography: a human volcano
- modern foreign languages: a translator
- drama: a mime
- PE: an internal organ
- art: a famous artist
- child development: a child of a particular developmental age
- PSHE: a drug addict.

Mission Impossible

Never underestimate the power of the envelope and all its pregnant promises. We can try to deny it, but we all know deep down how exciting it is to receive a sealed envelope that clearly isn't a bill or a circular. Any individual or pair activity to start the lesson can be immediately pimped by presenting the task as a secret mission, carefully sealed in intriguing packaging. Not only will the pupils be touched by the lovingly wrapped secrets, but your observer will be impressed by your beyond-the-call-of-duty innovation too. Moreover, you can gain an A* for your differentiation by providing missions which differ in complexity and which could be distributed according to ability.

The following are offered simply as examples of how this might work in various subjects:

- English: matching quotes with characters
- science: a mistake-spotting activity
- maths: matching fractions with decimals
- geography: True or False sorting activity
- history: a sequence of events to order
- PSHE/citizenship: sorting statements in order of perceived importance.

The Rule in the Room

This is a great trick for introducing a new skill in an amusing and engaging way. While one pupil waits outside the classroom, the remaining pupils are given a rule which will govern their behaviour and their responses to questions when the first pupil returns to the room. On re-entering the room, the first pupil must ask random questions about her classmates' lives, experiences, preferences, etc. The rest of the class respond to these questions while simultaneously adhering to the 'rule in the room'.

This starter can be adapted to introduce themes, ideas and physical skills. The following are just a few cross-curricular examples of ways this game can be used to illuminate a topic:

- English: participants must use alliteration in their speech
- science: participants must incorporate a word that can be associated with digestion
- maths: participants must include a prime number somewhere in their response
- MFL: participants must exclusively use the future tense in their responses
- PSHE/citizenship: participants must use body language which shows they are aggressive/on drugs/a bully, etc

5 × 5 Blockbusters

This one is not for the faint-hearted because it requires pupils to be on their feet and possibly reorganization of the classroom to provide space. For this lively activity, you need large laminated cards featuring the first letters of various keywords. These letters are then placed on the floor, face up to form a 5 × 5 square. The class is split into two teams who each select one representative to stand at adjacent edges of the square. One team must cross the square vertically and one horizontally. Each team selects the letter they wish their representative to stand on. The teams must answer a question which leads to the subject-specific word signified by the chosen letter. If they respond accurately, the letter is turned face-down and they may stand on it. The opposing team is henceforth blocked from using it for their own journey across the square, and must find an alternative route. Teams may not jump squares and must arrive first at the opposite side from the one they started on in order to win the game.

The questions – which would normally be posed by the teacher – can, of course, vary in complexity. Pupils might simply be asked to spell or define a subject-specific word which begins with the chosen letter, or they might be required to recall a specific term learned in a previous lesson.

Figure 12.1 illustrates how this starter activity might work in a number of different subjects.

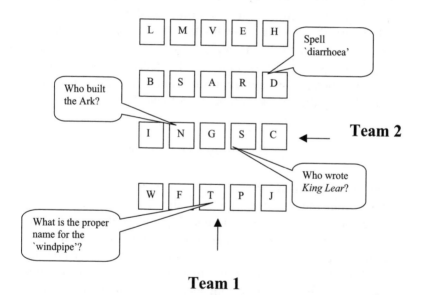

Figure 12.1

Coloured cards

You have probably seen this approach on one of those model lesson videos for teachers, tried it a couple of times and decided the ostentatious whizziness of it just isn't worth the total chaos and irritating excitement it causes among the pupils. The secret, however, is to persevere until the little darlings get over their initial hysteria and the novelty becomes a familiar, lively activity. Each pupil is given a set of different coloured cards which, if at all possible, should be coloured on one side and either plain black or plain white on the other. This prevents students from instantly copying the colour that they see all the hands in front of them raise. A particular response such as True or False or perhaps the names of characters can be assigned to each colour and written up on the board for pupils to refer to. The teacher then fires questions at the group and pupils must hold up the card which represents the correct answer. This activity can provide an enjoyable alternative to a simple Q+A session in any subject. It also allows you to assess, in a very immediate and visual way, exactly which pupils have understood and which have not. (And you can pop that in the AfL section of your lesson plan!)

Little wipeable boards

These can be used in a very similar way to the coloured cards (see above), but the added advantage is that the pupils can write a more specific response on the board before holding it up. This allows for an unlimited number of responses rather than the two or three represented by the assigned colours. It should be pointed out, however, that it takes far longer to scan the pupils' written responses than it does to distinguish between different coloured cards. By the way, if your school is on a tight budget and not yet initiated into the joys of little wipeable boards, you can laminate pieces of card. They are not quite as easily 'wipeable' as their melamine superiors but they are at least scrubbable.

Mind the Gap!

This amusing game offers another opportunity to use the wipeable boards and is a super-pimp version of cloze procedure. The teacher shows or reads to the class a statement or quotation, but removes one word from the text. Pupils must hold up suggested words to insert in the gap. This exercise might require them to recall key vocabulary, simply make sense of a sentence or show impressive familiarity with a text. If you are in the right mood, you might allow them to occasionally suggest a less probable word or phrase, for the sake of comic relief . . .

Bumps (not necessarily musical)

Ever noticed how some kids love to stand up and sit down again for no apparent reason? They'll tell you that they were tucking their shirts in or stretching, but the truth is, kids just like bouncing. That's why the guy who invented space hoppers is a millionaire. So here's a way to get 'bottoms on chairs' faster than you've ever managed it before and combine it with some serious revision and assessment.

Starting with the whole class standing, you will need to read a text aloud to them and ask them to identify examples of a particular concept as they listen to it. Each time they believe they have heard an example of the given focus, they must sit down immediately in their chairs. This allows you to instantly see who understands and who does not. As in Musical Bumps, pupils can be eliminated if they sit at the wrong time or fail to sit at the correct moment. This exercise can sometimes lend itself to music. For example, in an English lesson, pupils might listen to a well-known pop song and sit down every time they hear a proper noun. In MFL they might be required to sit each time they hear an infinitive verb . . .

Relays

Another one for kinesthetic learners, this starter works especially well with small classes. The classroom board is divided into two halves and the same text is written or projected onto each half in clear, easily legible script. Two teams of around five pupils stand at the back of the classroom in two queues. When the teacher signals the start of the relay, the pupils at the front of each queue move to the board, identify a mistake in the text and insert the correction. The same pupil must then return to their queue and hand the board pen to the next person in the team, before they, in turn, move forwards to the board to continue the relay.

However, if the very idea of pupils possibly *running* in your classroom sends a cold hand of horror creeping round your heart, you can allow each team to stand next to the board so that only a little movement is required. The possibilities for incorporating relays into your lesson are endless. For example, you could have a series of maths problems on the board and each leg of the relay must answer, or correct the answer, to one problem; the relay finishes when all problems are answered correctly. In English, you could write out a passage on the board with rampant spelling and grammar errors and have the relay teams correct them in the same fashion as the previous example. In a science lesson, you could put a diagram of the human body on the board, and have team members race up to label or annotate features of the nervous system.

Role Reversal

For full details about how this strategy can be used, flip back to Chapter 4. As a starter, this well-known 'teacher-makes-a-prat-of-herself' activity allows you to fully entertain the observer as well as your class, while immediately conveying very clear learning objectives. In fact, if your pupils are successful in identifying what you needed to do in order to achieve your aim, then it is they themselves who establish the objectives for their own learning in the first ten minutes of the lesson. Clever, huh?

Even if it means wracking your brains for a little while, we are confident that there is no subject that this starter will not adapt to. So have fun, and if you get stuck, you might want to model yourself on one of your less endearing pupils – just don't make it too obvious ...!

Checklist

1. The starter should last approximately 10 minutes. Do not allow it to take over the lesson.
2. Make it clear to the pupils the purpose of the activity and what you want them to have achieved by the end of it. Lavish praise on them when they get it right. (This gives them a warm fuzzy glow while simultaneously flagging up your own triumph to the observer!)
3. Plan for the frustrating inevitability of latecomers. Organize a starter which can be quickly understood and picked up by any pupils joining the class after your exposition. A brief outline of the task could appear on any resources or alternatively on the board.

Trash it!

Steer your pimpmobile well clear of these overused and abused archaisms. They're not clever, and they're not funny.

- **Wordsearches** handed out as pupils enter the classroom. OK, so we all know this can ensure a very quiet and *apparently* purposeful start to the lesson, but really, how much learning will actually take place here? It's utterly unimaginative. Don't do it.
- **Written spelling tests.** This is not only a painfully uninspiring starter, it's also just plain mean. Just because all your lessons began like this when you were a pupil, doesn't mean you have to take it out on the next generation. Refer back to the pimped-up starters for some innovative ways to spice up this punishing practice.

- **Totally irrelevant, unconnected activities.** Yes, there may well be an old reliable, tried and tested activity that you know will be well received by pupils, but seriously, if you have to add an extra chapter in your lesson plan to justify how your starter relates to the rest of the lesson, then think of something different. Similarly, don't just pull a 'ready-to-photocopy' starter out of your 'Ready-to Photocopy Starters' book. It doesn't suggest a great familiarity or level of comfort with the whole concept.

> A teacher's constant task is to take a room full of live wires and see to it that they're grounded.
>
> E.C. McKenzie

Your Sky Box goes on the fritz five minutes before the end of CSI and you never get to know who robbed the casino. Your DVD player dies right before Patrick Swayze is able to say 'Nobody puts Baby in a corner', and they 'Dirty Dance' themselves into our hearts forever. Your TV starts to smoke and you are forced to turn it off right before Lampard scores the game-winning goal that EVERYONE is talking about in the staffroom the next day. Dinner with no dessert. New Year's day with no hangover. Laundry with no tumble dryer. Yes, life goes on and you find a way to muddle through without these critical moments and devices, but let's face it: they all go hand in hand.

Plenaries are a similar beast to these scenarios: you can plan and deliver the most brilliant lesson on the planet, but if you don't put the icing on that cake and remind the students of what they have just been taught, odds are that much of it may go the way of Mr T's career after *The A-Team* and disappear into obscurity. The pedagogical benefits of a plenary are not the only thing to keep in mind; one also needs to remember that the observer at the back of the room will be keeping their eagle-eyes peeled for this momentous event that will tie your lesson together. No plenary, no 'Outstanding'. It's as simple as that.

The catch-22 of the plenary is that when your lesson is going swimmingly and students are responding really well to a task you have set, or if your lesson is going remarkably badly and your students 'just don't get it' and are taking ten times longer than you expected to complete a task, the default part of the lesson to scrap is the plenary – simply because you run out of time. Big mistake. The little gold nugget at the end of this chapter is a collection of top tips for how to avoid resorting to this cardinal sin.

When Ofsted first published their report of the Key Stage 3 Pilot in 2002, they reported that the plenary was 'often the weakest part of the lesson' and 'often the least active part of the lesson'. Yikes. Your plenary needs to be more than just you reimparting your brilliance to the students. The way to make it memorable – 'Outstanding' even – is to have the students tell you what they have learned and actively participate in reminding themselves and others in the room of what they have just accomplished. Some of Ofsted's suggestions (www.dfes.gov.uk) about what plenaries could be used for are:

- to draw together what has been learned; to highlight the most important rather than the most recent points; to summarize key facts, ideas and vocabulary; and to stress what needs to be remembered
- to generalize from examples generated earlier in the lesson
- to go through an exercise, question pupils and rectify any remaining misunderstandings
- to make links between other work and what the class will go on to do next
- to highlight not only what pupils have learned, but also how they have learned it
- to highlight the progress pupils have made and remind them about their personal targets
- to set homework to extend or consolidate classwork and prepare for future lessons.

Now let's put those suggestions into practice . . .

Jazzy W. Bushmaster adjusted the faux-fur collar on his blingin' suit and reached for the lavender memo peeking from his pigeon-hole. Lavender memos were never good news. Sure enough, the mauve menace was forewarning him of the SLT observation he had been expecting ever since Ofsted had raised some concerns about the department, just a fortnight before. All members of the department had balked at Ofsted's criticism of lesson pace and structure in the two MFL lessons they had observed.

Jazzy knew that he had to show the SLT that the inspectors were incorrect and had just been observing the wrong lessons. They had missed out on his

pimptacular teaching methods and pace. He needed the baddest lesson plan with the maddest strategies this ol' headteacher had ever seen. He knew that the way to ace that observation was to ensure the plenary was, shall we say, spectaculaire.

Jazzy obviously knows that making time for a fabulous plenary is the best way to show his observer his optimal time-management and planning skills. The following are some strategies we shared with Jazzy to guarantee he would 'wow' his headteacher.

Plenary Pals

For full details of this strategy, check out Chapter 4. In short, this strategy passes the buck of facilitating the plenary to members of your class on a rota basis. Not surprisingly, many plenary strategies have strong links to AfL; you may find several strategies in Chapter 4 that will assist in the pimptabulous planning of your plenary!

Grandma's Trunk

This strategy is borrowed from games played on long car journeys taken as a child. For 'Grandma's Trunk', the strategy begins with one student completing the statement 'When I opened Grandma's trunk I found …', filling in the blank with an object, keyword, character, important date/fact/skill, etc. that is pertinent to the lesson you have just taught or the topic being covered in general. The next student is to repeat the statement and example that the first student has contributed and add one of their own. The third student repeats and adds, and so on and so forth until a student can no longer remember the sequence. Though it does involve some rote memorization, it definitely reinforces key terms and facets of a topic for the class that have minds like sieves. It has a strong element of competition, with the class wanting to outdo their last effort or perhaps that of a parallel group.

You can 'up' the challenge of this strategy by asking students to add an important fact, or qualify the item they are putting into Grandma's trunk. For example, in a Year 8 history lesson on the Battle of Hastings, rather than allowing the students to say, 'When I opened Grandma's trunk I found Harald Hardrada, Senlac Hill, and an eye with an arrow through it', you could insist upon a qualifying comment to accompany each item. This might sound something like: 'When I opened Grandma's trunk I found Harald Hardrada (the guy from Norway and Denmark who thought he had a claim through his ancestors), Senlac Hill (the place where William finally kicked Harold's butt) and an arrow through the eye ('cos that's how Harold Godwinson died).'

Rather than just adding an item to the end of the list, you could also keep your students on their toes with this method by posing a question that the next 'victim' will have to answer. You could definitely use the beach ball covered in Chapter 12 for this activity as well: whoever catches the beach ball is the next to look inside Grandma's trunk ...

Flyswatter

This widely used technique is the ideal way to put all those extra flyswatters you have hanging around the house to great use. (You DO have loads of extra flyswatters at home, don't you ...?) A series of keywords or short phrases drawn from the lesson are placed at random on the board. Divide your class in two and choose a delegate from each side of the classroom to grab a 'flyswatter' and stand at the back of the room. (You will need a centre aisle that is free from any tripping hazards.) You ask a question and the two delegates must race to the front and 'swat' the correct answer. The loser passes their swatter on to someone else on their team and the winner retains their swatter. It is a good idea to put a limit on the number of turns a swatter can have; team mates will definitely get bored if they don't see the possibility of a turn in the near future.

This activity is great fun and gets students (especially your kinesthetic learners!) excited and involved in the plenary. You could give the class some ownership of the activity by having students generate the keywords to go on the board together; two or three suggestions per pair will give you plenty to choose from. You could also give this strategy a twist by putting the questions on the board and calling out the answer instead.

Cookie Monster

I'm sure we can all think back to the glory days of children's television and remember good old *Sesame Street* and, specifically, that lovely blue lunker, Cookie Monster. Dig a little bit deeper and think back to his wonderful little segment where they would, for example, put a bunch of dancing apples on the page and one dancing orange and sing, 'One of these things is not like the other thing, one of these things just doesn't belong . . .'

If you can get a copy of the song, many classes think it is quite funny and quickly remember the premise. You choose a series of three to four statements, objects, key terms, characters, etc. and either put them on the board or read them to the class. The class's task is to identify which does not belong. It can add an element of competition and fun if you can actually play the song (or any other) for the time that you want the students to be contemplating their response.

The really outstanding part of this strategy is that there isn't necessarily a correct answer every time and students get quite excited about offering their twist on the puzzle. It encourages higher-level thinking and is a great way for them to consider carefully what they have learned that lesson. To really test them, have them develop, in pairs or small groups, their own 'Cookie Monster Challenge' to share with the class.

What have I learned?

This is a simple strategy that is really easy to prepare and even easier to deliver because the onus is put almost entirely on the students. This strategy can be part of classroom routine; if the students already know the questions and the format of this strategy then they will more effectively respond to the self-reflection. This strategy is based around posing them four simple questions:

1. What did you learn this lesson that you did not know before?
2. Which part of the lesson did you most enjoy?
3. Which part of the lesson could you use a bit more help with?
4. Which of your achievements are you most proud of this lesson?

While this strategy may not be oozing with bells and whistles or singing and dancing, this is a very clear way for students to reflect on their learning. It is also an excellent way for you to see what has been clearly understood by the class and what might need some revision and attention the following lesson. So long as your head of department is not on an anti-photocopying campaign, you could design a worksheet for this that students will glue in their books upon completion, and you could keep a supply of them to hand any time you need a quick plenary. They can also be used as part of a homework task.

Scavenger Hunt

This strategy can be used effectively in several different ways, each obviously depending on the size of your class and classroom and on the materials you have available. The first, and probably safest, way of using this strategy is to have a section of text, picture, source document, model, etc. in which you have identified specific features. You provide the class with the list of features that you want them to find in the sample and they go about locating them.

The second means of using this strategy involves your placing at random spots around the room, answers to questions provided by you. Students must locate the answers to the questions in the not-so-secret locations around the room and detail the answer, as well as where they found it in order to gain credit for their 'find'. Your answers may be 'hidden' inside relevant textbooks, on pertinent displays, or, if ICT facilities are available, on websites or the school intranet. In small classrooms or with big classes this quickly becomes difficult to have students wandering around the room looking for things (and it can be asking to create a mess). To avoid this potential catastrophe, you can, before the lesson, post the answers on the walls around the room, on different coloured cards. When students are recording their answers they need only indicate the colour of the card they found the appropriate answer on. Odds are, they will have taken notice of them earlier in the lesson, and this can create a great element of mystery while the class tries to figure out what the random statements on the wall pertain to.

This strategy is very effective as it is easily differentiated for different groups and the healthy element of competition engages and involves all students in the class. It can also be done on an individual, paired or group basis, affording a great deal of flexibility.

Sound Collage

A twist on the cut and paste versions using largely images, a 'Sound Collage' relies on powerful or significant statements made and shared at random in the lesson. This strategy works best with subjective, creative and opinion-based assignments, but you can certainly adapt it to fit nearly any situation or topic. Sound Collage is an excellent plenary to use if you are short on time, as it shouldn't take much more than ten minutes to complete.

With about two minutes left of the class's working time, ask students to stop and read through their work to find a sentence, phrase or powerful word that they feel best summarizes the point they have made or feelings they have expressed, and underline it. At the end of the two minutes, ask the class to put their heads on their desks or close their eyes (many groups are suspicious of this, we know!) and instruct them that if they feel a tap on their shoulder to read out the sentence, phrase or word they have underlined. Move around the classroom at random, tapping the shoulders of as many students as you feel is necessary to convey the message. Once finished, ask students to sit up and feed back about the variety of messages they heard. Was there a common theme? Did any in particular stand out or not fit in?

This strategy is an excellent way to involve a significant number of students in a short plenary and it gives many students the opportunity to share only the best of their work without feeling self-conscious about the final product.

Pass the Parcel

Again, let's take you back to your childhood: this time, a birthday party. What was more exciting than that moment when the music stopped, the parcel was in your hand and you got to peel off a coveted layer of the passing-parcel? Fabulous. Your class will think so too when you blow them away with your 'Pass the Parcel' plenary. Though this takes a little bit of fiddly preparation, it is a great deal of fun that your class, and your inspector, will be keen to get involved in.

The layers of your parcel will alternate between one containing a question/task and one containing a small prize (sweets are obviously the easiest, although if your inspector is Jamie Oliver, you should probably use little boxes of raisins). When the music is playing, the parcel is being passed; when the music stops, the student with the parcel unwraps a layer. If they can answer the question or complete the task, they are allowed to unwrap the next layer and take the prize. If they do not, they must pass the task and the parcel on to the next student. You can be as creative as you like with the kinds of challenges you put in the parcel and tailor them for the kinds of activities you know your class best responds to. Show off a good relationship with your class to your observer by adding funny qualifiers to your task; for example, 'Explain the role of saliva in digestion; sing your answer to the tune of "Row, Row, Row Your Boat".' Making the class, and hopefully your observer, smile, or even laugh, is an excellent tone to end the lesson on, not to mention a fun way of summarizing the learning.

Starter Stars!

A spin on 'Plenary Pals', this strategy gets your class to have a hand in planning the starter activity for their next lesson on the premise that they will need to recap skills acquired this lesson in the following one. You can make the task as creative or prescriptive as you wish. You may want to set down specific guidelines for what the starter must include, or specify the format of it, or you may want to encourage students to be creative and use a method of their choice. This will obviously be dependent on what you already know of your group's abilities; you don't want a class whose forte isn't creativity to be giving you blank stares because you haven't given them clear guidelines about what they must do. Ensure that they all submit a written plan for their starter activity so that you are able to assess their learning and what they have taken, or failed to take, from the lesson. Choose one, possibly two if you feel it is appropriate, to actually use as a starter the following lesson. You may choose to deliver it yourself or have the group that designed it to do the 'delivering'.

You do not get the immediate feedback that many of the other strategies provide, but this strategy is great for giving your class a sense of ownership of their lessons. You are still able to assess what the students have learned, and they are still recapping the important points of their lesson. You will need to be explicit when you draw their attention to the learning objective and the key points that their plenary should include.

Sell This Product!

This strategy is often used in English lessons when teaching media and persuasive language, but can easily be adapted to fit any discipline. The strategy is simple: students, who have vast experience of being exposed to advertising and persuasion, are given an object/person/event/concept that they must 'sell' to the class. This is really just another means of asking the students to identify the important features of any given idea or concept. For example, you may ask your GCSE history class working towards their Medicine through Time coursework to 'sell' insulin to a group of sceptics, explaining its origins and benefits; your Year 9 maths class to choose a buyer to 'sell' Pythagoras' theorem to (there are too many markets that would be interested to list them all here!); or perhaps your GCSE resistant materials class could 'sell' their plans for a coffee table to Ikea.

For those classes that might struggle to grasp the finer points of salesmanship, you could be well served to put into practice some AfL principles (we told you there would be overlap, didn't we!) and provide them with some sentence stems they must include in their sales pitch, such as:

- 'Our product is like no other because ...'
- 'Your company needs to purchase our product because ...'
- 'This product will revolutionize (insert appropriate cause) with its ...'
- 'Benefits of this ground-breaking invention are ...'

Providing a list of select key terms that they must include is also an excellent application of AfL and will elicit the kind of responses both you and your observer will be hoping for.

The Little Gold Nugget ...

So, you've planned the perfect lesson, complete with approximate timings, and know in your heart of hearts it will be the best lesson you have ever taught, when (infuriatingly):

- that blasted starter activity takes fifteen minutes instead of five;
- you need to recap on necessary information that you THOUGHT they had grasped by now (how many times DO you have to teach them how to conjugate the verb 'avoir'??);
- the most disruptive and aggravating child in the universe has delayed the progress of your lesson through their shoddy behaviour;

135

- the year group assembly was let out ten minutes late, consequently throwing your carefully planned timings out the window (which you only wish, at times like this, would open wide enough to throw *yourself* out of);
- moments before the lesson is due to begin, two girls from your tutor group have come to tell you (in floods of greyish-black tears) that their lives are over and they can't attend any lessons because their boyfriend (you know, the boy with the long hair and the trousers that are always so low you can see his grotty pants) has dumped them for that tart in Mrs Jones' form and now everyone is talking about them so what can they possibly do today besides sit in the toilets and cry and contemplate sick and twisted means of revenge on the tart because it's all her fault anyways because she was totally trying to pull him at Jamie Wilson's party at the weekend and everyone knows that he's only doing it because she's easy anyways ... And by the time you have calmed them down and convinced them that (like Cher says) there's life after love, you are five minutes late starting your lesson.

If it's not one of these charming scenarios, it's another. You know that because of the delay, at one point or another, you will not be able to stick to your meticulous plan; something has got to go. This next point cannot be stressed enough: It Must Not Be Your Plenary. The following are some ideas of ways to make up time so the crucial moment of the plenary need not be skipped:

- If the students' individual task for the lesson involves a written task, have them write only the opening paragraph (or two, whatever there is time for), but highlight specifically the things you want to see in the abbreviated form of the assignment. Tell the class this is what you want them to do so that both they and your observer are clear about the volume of work expected of them and do not feel disappointed that they have not squeezed in a point that is significant to them.
- Scrap the point in the lesson where pupils share examples of what they have done in the main body of the lesson; they can show you what they have learned through the plenary.

- Have the students tackle the main task in pairs, rather than as individuals; two heads SHOULD be quicker than one.
- Talk through as a class, solutions/ideas for formative questions and have students work through the more challenging ones.

Trash it!

Old dogs might not do new tricks, but here are a few tricks we need those old dogs to forget!

Bog-standard teacher-led Q&A sessions

This is perfectly adequate for an everyday bog-standard lesson where you are just doing a quick check at the end to ensure that students did not sleep through your riveting reading (complete with dubious accent) of *Of Mice and Men*, but when you are out to impress, or really hit a point home, this simply will not do.

The Traffic Light System

OK, OK, we get it: it's a 'great' visual representation of whether a child has grasped the day's lesson or not. Yes, we understand that it is frequently successful in the primary sector when children leave a 'dot' at the end of their work to show how they feel about it. But let's think in practical terms: who wants to be the wally holding up a red card in a sea of green ones? What child is going to confidently hold their yellow card high when their mate beside them is showing the self-assured green one? Who wants to have a roomful of children armed with sharp red pencils if the lesson did not go down as well as you had hoped? Let's face it: in most classes, the traffic lights should have their proverbial bulbs unscrewed. If you are really hung up on this method, check out the 'Role Reversal' strategy in Chapter 4 for a souped-up version of this stale cracker.

A selection of students reading out their work

This is the classroom equivalent to going to your mate's house and being subjected to looking through reams and reams of holiday photos. Most children, though keen to read out their own work to prove their brilliance, do not actually care what the person beside them has written down. Aspects of it, sure, but to have five children read out their near-identical responses to a written task is, quite frankly, a lesson killer.

Going through answers

Yes, you need to share the answers to let your students know whether they have hit the mark or not, but this does not HAVE to be the culminating event of your lesson. It doesn't even have to happen in the lesson; you could go through your own marking of their work. These precious moments at the end of the lesson can be much better spent than announcing 'The answer to number 4 is . . .'.

Around 52.5 million people tuned in for the airing of the last episode of *Friends* in 2004 and there's a good reason for it: it's the ending that counts. Your plenary is the last thing your students will take away from the lesson and the last thing your observer will be assessing you on. It's make or break, baby. Have a bit of fun and make it enjoyable; there's a very good reason that there are no desserts known to humankind that contain Brussels sprouts. Remember that . . .

> The mediocre teacher tells. The good teacher explains. The superior teacher demonstrates. The great teacher inspires.
>
> William Arthur Ward

We have a dream. We have a dream that teachers the world over will one day be able to join hands and hearts and unashamedly pimp their lessons to the nth degree and do it without sacrificing their beauty sleep and without raising suspicion among their colleagues. We have a dream that Ofsted inspectors, HoDs, SMTs, mentors, consultants and advisers will drop their jaws and their pens when they see the pimptastic ways that teachers break their backs to make their lessons outstanding. We have a dream that lesson plans, resources, starters, plenaries and any initiative that comes barrelling down the pike will be digested, regurgitated and transformed by the pimping masses who will receive merit and recognition for doing so. We have a dream today. We have a dream that students in classrooms around the country will bask in the innovation, excitement and unique learning opportunities provided to them by their pimping teachers and will absorb and utilize this learning to better themselves and the world. We have a dream today.

Much like those salsa-dancing lessons you took last autumn the art of pimping your lessons needs practice, needs nurture and needs expansion. Don't hold yourself back or save your flair for the one big day a year you strut your stuff; weave it into the fabric of your everyday being. Spread the gospel of pimping, share your applications and uses of it with your department or even faculty. We have all felt our creativity wells run dry; so share your new ideas with your colleagues and eventually, with luck, your teaching karma will reward you with reciprocal gems.

You can't make an omelette without breaking a few eggs (just try to count the clichés in this book, we dare you) so if you give a strategy or two a try and they are a big giant flop, don't stress, it does not mean that you can't pimp; it just means you have to try, try again. Like we mentioned at the outset, outstanding lessons are about taking risks and not just digging the same old project out of the cupboard and delivering it in the same old way. There is always room for same and old ... that is why we are not all fired at the end of each year and replaced with fresh, enthusiastic NQTs. To improve your own sanity and to keep you fresh, you simply must make room for the pimped.

If you have bought this book AND read all the way to the end then you have already shown that you are interested in shaking off the dust and shaking up your lessons. For those sceptics out there that resent and reject anything to do with flash cards, laminating and colour-coding, fear not and read again ... there's plenty for you in here as well. Pimping does not have to become silly and does not have to get out of control. And you don't have to wear gold chains or velour. We only said that because we thought it was funny ...

To send you on your way to pimping your lessons, here's a little shopping list of items you will require. Most of these pimping accessories can be found in those teacher-friendly 'Everything's a Pound' shop, but make sure you keep the receipt for your school accountant ...

- An array of flyswatters (see Chapter 13)
- A beach ball (see Chapters 12 and 13)
- Two-tone coloured card (preferably black or white on the back, coloured on the front) (see Chapter 12)
- Thousands of highlighters (see Chapters 4 and 13)
- A copy of 'Sesame Street Sings', or some other motivational music (see Chapter 13)
- Wrapping paper (see Chapter 13)
- A sackful of envelopes.

In observation situations, it is never *good luck* over *good planning* and though your pimping will undoubtedly become a part of your routine this is not to say that you can become complacent when it comes to demonstrating what you can do. Make the most of your opportunity to shine and ensure that you have planned, and planned again and prepared, and prepared again for the best- and the worst-case scenarios. To all those nay-sayers out there that reject the notion of observation and become irritable at the idea that they should do anything more than they would normally do, we reject and are irritable with you. Why, oh why, would you deny an opportunity to show how brilliant you can be in the most explicit way possible? Unless, of course, it is because you aren't very brilliant in the first place. You would never wear trackie bottoms to the Queen's house for dinner, you would never neglect to brush your teeth before going to the dentist and you would never tell rude jokes in front of your partner's parents the first time you meet them. Why? Because you want to put your best foot forward before the Queen sees that you chew with your mouth open, the dentist finds out you have cavities and your partner's parents find out that you have an unhealthy sense of humour when it comes to jokes involving flatulence. Your opportunities (yes, opportunities, not torture sessions) for observation should be embraced with the same attitude of aiming to impress.

No matter how hard we try, we can't downright disapprove of school inspections, of quality assurance or performance-management observations. After all, we need to know that what we teachers are doing is important enough for someone to bother checking up on. When we were first set loose on the paints at nursery school, would we have taken such delight if we knew that no one wanted to see the painting we produced? And don't you have a sneaky suspicion that the *Big Brother* contestants would be painfully boring and just plain nice if there were no cameras watching them?

If you have heard teachers say, 'This observation programme is ridiculous! Why can't we just be trusted to do a good job? We are professionals, for goodness sake!', tell them to try working in a school where they are never observed – *ever*. Certainly, it might seem liberating at first; you might well begin to enjoy the freedom of being able to pull your lessons out of your ear and leave that pile of marking to gather a little dust. But after a while, if you are a good teacher, the likelihood is it will begin to get you down. Do people really not care what you're like? Are you, to all intents and purposes, sharing the same category as that insipid colleague down the corridor who spends most of her teaching time on eBay while her pupils complete wordsearches from 'teachcrap.com'?

If they are still unconvinced, tell them about a colleague of ours who was an excellent teacher in the classroom but terrible at getting round to doing his marking. Loved though he was by his pupils, one day an entire class mutinously declared that they did not 'see the point of writing the essays if he wasn't going to mark them'. You have to admit that they kind of had a point. That's human nature. It's not about whether you like to be under the Ofsted microscope or not; it's about knowing that somebody cares one way or the other about how well you are working. Deny it if you like, but the truth is, when you value what you do and the outcomes you produce, you crave professional feedback and validation just as much as the next applause junkie.

And yes, like it or not, some teachers have been made junkies of the four-point scale. At first it was mildly interesting but now they cannot do without it. An observation report with no overall numerical assessment? It's unthinkable. Observation as a valuable tool for the ongoing process of self-evaluation? Tosh. A young colleague recently admitted that on receiving detailed, constructive feedback from her external AST assessor after a gruelling day of observations and interviews, she suddenly burst out, 'OK, cut the bollocks, man – what number did I get?'!

We can all remember our best teachers. It is one of those dreadfully cheesy, but unavoidable facts that, decades later, the teachers who really inspired us to learn, still occupy a vivid part of our memory, despite our inability to remember the postcode of the establishment we work at from one day to the next. The chances are, those teachers didn't enhance your numeracy skills, stretch your potential, meet all your spiritual needs, plan a plenary, while spinning brightly coloured resources on sticks and juggling three AfL techniques all at the same time, in *every single lesson*. Did you love them any the less for it? The question that remains then is what does 'outstanding teaching' really mean?

We have laid great emphasis, in this book, on the phenomenon of the observation lesson and on the government's complex and slippery definition of an 'outstanding lesson'. The terrible truth lies exposed before us. Let us all admit to it together: it is impossible to be this version of *outstanding* all of the time. The first step to salvation is saying it out loud. If we were to take every criterion for *outstanding teaching* and cram them all into one big, shining statue of outstanding teacherness, before which to prostrate ourselves in awe, it would be a skyscraping monstrosity.

In the preceding chapters, we have seen that in order to be an *outstanding* teacher, we must also be prepared to play the role of a health adviser, a lifeguard, a life-coach, a guru, an actor, a designer, a mathematician, a linguist (we can feel a novelty t-shirt coming on), a technician, a financial adviser, a comedian and much, much more.

However, if by 'outstanding' we mean *dedicated*; if we mean *enthusiastic, hard-working, passionate*; if 'outstanding' relates to the number of young people we inspire to take their learning further and not to the number of government initiatives we embrace, then you were probably jolly-damn outstanding before you even read this book. And you don't need some power-tripping observer to tell you that.

So go ahead. Take your badass pimping techniques out onto the streets. Go forth and spread the pimping trend until lessons across the country are transformed; until pupils queue outside the school gates like fans at a pop concert; until students no longer waste their pocket money on yet another MP3 player, but instead offer it up in exchange for extra tuition. Go forth and pimpify . . .

Index

argue, 59, 80, 90, 92–3
Assessment for Learning (AfL),
   43–7, 50–6, 143
   and lesson plan, 34–5
   and plenaries, 128, 135
   and preparation, 26
   and resources, 104
   and starter activities, 120
AST assessment, 31, 143
attendance. 36, 77

Bloom's Taxonomy, 78, 85

Citizenship, 37, 58, 117–18
cloze, 49, 91, 121
Colour-Coded Compliments, 45, 52
competition, 50, 128, 130, 132
criteria, 27, 144
   and assessment, 44–5, 49–53,
      80, 114
   and effective teaching, 11, 16, 20
curriculum, 5, 17–19, 62, 82, 95

DfES, 32, 95, 114, 127
Differentiation, 26, 30, 34, 38,
   72–79, 81, 83, 85–6, 114, 117

English, 38, 41, 49, 51, 84, 116–8,
   lessons, 31, 36, 82, 99, 121–2,
      134
   teachers, 31, 34, 70, 99,

evaluation, 25, 34, 37, 40, 45–6,
   50–2, 58, 63, 80, 143
Every Child Matters (ECM), 33,
   66–7, 69, 70–1

FEET, 93

GCSE, 31, 37–8, 43, 135,
goals, 4–5, 50
grade, 14–15, 25, 54, 109, 113
grammar, 89, 91, 122

homework, 89, 100–1, 114, 127,
   131
   and assessment, 49–50, 54,
   family, 63
   and lesson plan, 36, 39, 40
   and preparation, 14–16, 18,
      21–2

ICT, 26, 34, 99–102, 132
Individual Education Plan, 12, 21,
   22
Inspection Report, 9–10
interview lesson, 25

Keyword Feedback, 45, 51–2
kinaesthetic, 38, 51, 67–8, 81, 122,
   129

Latin, 5

learning outcomes, 33, 37
lesson objective, 32–3, 39, 46
lesson plan, 29–37, 39, 41, 44, 58, 63, 69, 127
  and differentiation, 73, 77, 81
  and literacy, 88, 91
  and numeracy, 95–6
  and preparation, 3, 9, 11, 15, 22
  and starter activities, 114, 120, 124
level, 14, 44–5, 54–5, 63, 70, 78, 104, 109, 114, 124
literacy, 5, 26, 34, 36, 82, 88–93

mathematics, 31, 75, 95, 117–8, 122, 135,
modelling, 52, 88–9

National Strategy, 35, 113
NQT year, 5, 31, 141
numeracy, 5, 26, 31, 34, 36, 38, 73, 94–9, 99, 143

Ofsted, 2, 5, 9–10, 15, 19, 27, 31
  and inspector, 24
oral, 33, 39, 47, 49, 62, 81–2

PGCE, 19, 31
Photocopying, 6, 21, 27, 39, 102, 106, 108, 124, 131
plenary, 5, 14, 21, 47–8, 55, 90, 101, 125–138, 140, 143
  and lesson plans, 35, 38–40
  Pals, 47–8, 80, 85, 128, 134
PSHE, 80, 82, 117–8
punctuation, 89, 91

Qualifications & Curriculum Authority (QCA), 43, 50
Quality Assurance Lesson Observation, 20

resources, 14, 34–5, 38–9, 44, 58, 102, 103–11, 123, 140, 143
  and preparation, 16–7, 19, 21–2
Role Reversal, 48–9, 61, 122, 137

self-assessment, 45, 55
Senior Leadership Team, 10, 24
Social, Moral, Cultural, Spiritual (SMCS), 5, 33–4, 59–61, 63–4
special education needs (SEN), 12, 21, 32, 36, 78
spelling, 34, 89–91, 122–3
strategy, 3–4, 26, 36, 38–9, 61, 115, 122, 128–34, 137, 140
  and assessment, 45, 47, 50
  and differentiation, 34, 38, 77
  National, 35, 113
  and SMCS, 60
Success Sorting, 45, 50–1

targets, 12, 14, 33, 36, 45, 50, 76, 127
technical equipment, 24
The 10 Principles, 43, 46, 50

visual, 81–2, 109, 120, 137

Year 2, 31
Year 7, 23, 104
Year 8, 129
Year 9, 135